THE POWER PYRAMID

Also by Diane Tracy:

The First Book of Common-Sense Management

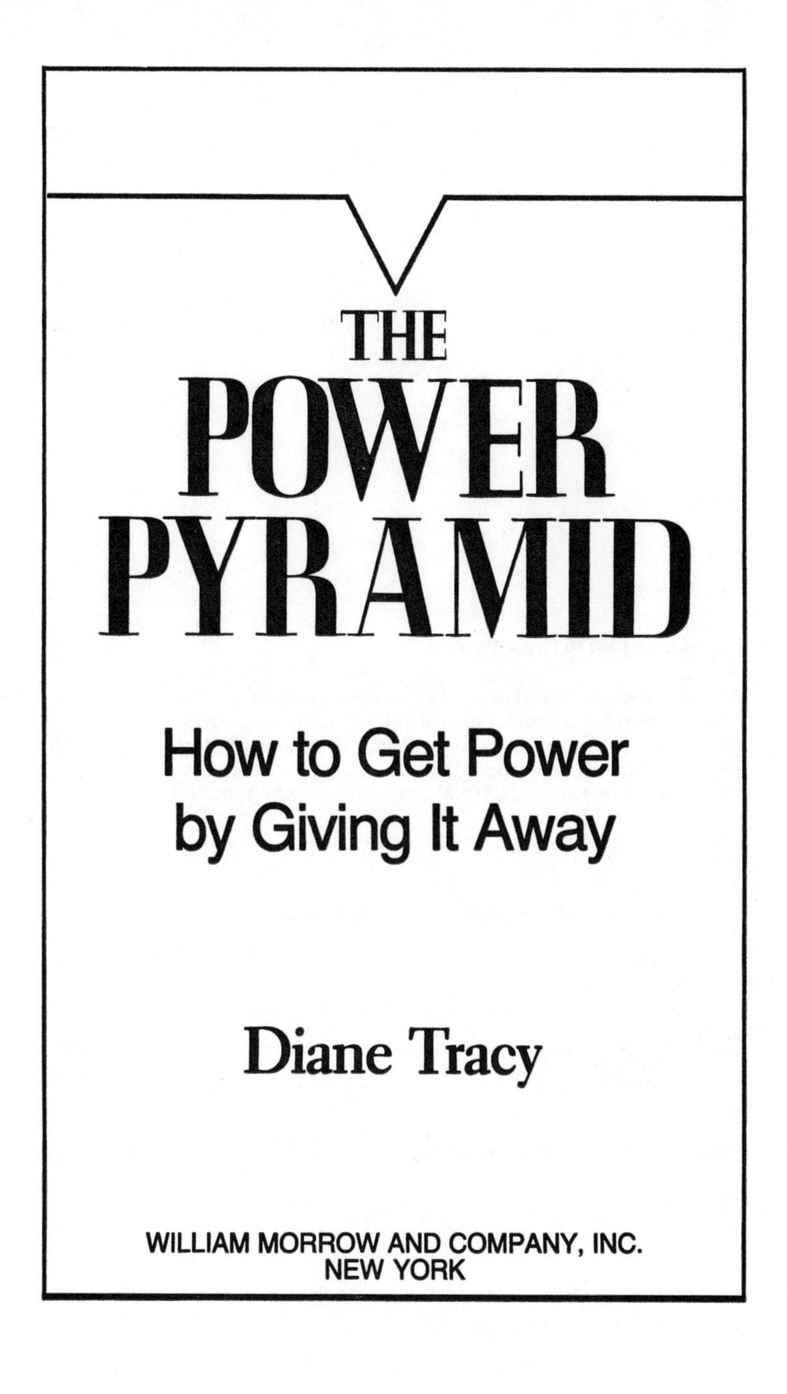

THE POWER PYRAMID

How to Get Power by Giving It Away

Diane Tracy

WILLIAM MORROW AND COMPANY, INC.
NEW YORK

Library of Congress Cataloging-in-Publication Data

Tracy, Diane.
The power pyramid: how to get power by giving it away/by Diane Tracy.
p. cm.
ISBN 0-688-08869-4
1. Supervision of employees. 2. Power (Social sciences) 3. Management
I. Title.
HF5549.12.T736 1990
658.4'07—dc20 89-12883
CIP

Printed in the United States of America

First Edition

1 2 3 4 5 6 7 8 9 10

BOOK DESIGN BY PATRICE FODERO

Contents

THE POWER PYRAMID

INTRODUCTION

Power. It is what everyone wants and no one seems to have enough of. World leaders, housewives, business executives, lovers—in search of that which will enable them to achieve their desired goals. The desire for power is inherent in our very nature and fundamental to our survival. Without it we could accomplish nothing.

The caveman invented fire, Napoleon conquered Europe, and Alexander Graham Bell invented the telephone, all for the same reason. Each wanted more power over his world. This universal quest for power helps shape history; it is one of the driving forces behind all human endeavor.

Nowhere is the pursuit of power more evident than in today's workplace. Managers are constantly striving to increase their arsenal of power, which is how it should be. Some may use power for selfish gain; others may use it to benefit the company. Regardless of how managers use power, the fact remains that without it they are incapable of achieving anything of significance for themselves, other people, the company, or society at large.

So the question is, "How do we get more power?" To answer we must first understand how power works. It operates under the same principle as love: The more one gives to others, the more one receives in return. Unfortunately, many managers assume that there is a limited supply of power; that giving power to another means diminishing one's own power.

This book tells how a manager can achieve ultimate power by giving power to the people who work for him. It shows how companies can unleash the vast storehouse of human potential that is untapped virtually everywhere in corporate America.

Most people contribute only a small fraction of their full capabilities, simply because they don't feel a sense of personal power. They are bound by a bureaucratic management system that does little to encourage initiative and high performance. Almost all the power within the organization rests with those at the very top. Powerless in their ability to achieve results, most people eventually lose interest and settle for mediocrity.

The secret of achieving success as a manager and as a company lies in learning how to release the hidden potential of people. It lies in helping workers on all levels, from floor sweeper to executive, experience a sense of their own power. There are no success limits for the managers who master this art. Likewise, the company that rewards managers for successfully employing this art dramatically increases its ability to achieve its objectives.

When we think of the word "power," a lot of images come to mind. Many people associate power with fear—as something that comes from on high to control and restrict them. Real power, however, works just the opposite way. It flows from the bottom up rather than from the top down. Ultimate power comes not by intimidating people with brute force, but by freeing them so that they can be all they can be.

A manager maximizes his own power and opportunity for success when he enables the people who work for him to achieve a sense of power and success.

The 10 Principles for Empowering People, which comprise what we call the Power Pyramid are described on the following pages. Based on age-old truths, they are simple, commonsense ideas, easy to understand yet powerful in their ability to achieve results.

The harder you work at applying each of these principles to the people who work for you, the greater the power you will have to achieve your own goals and objectives.

There is somewhat of a paradox involved here. And that is: If you want to achieve ultimate power for yourself you must get out of your own way. Instead of focusing your energies on the acquisition of power for yourself, focus them on how you can empower the people who work for you. If you are successful in giving your people power, they will surely lift you on their shoulders to heights of power and success you never dreamed possible.

NOTE: This is a book about equality and fairness for everyone, men and women alike. Therefore, I hope none will be offended by my use of the masculine gender, which has been used purely for the sake of readability.

CHAPTER

1

POWER THROUGH RESPONSIBILITY

Power Principle: A manager empowers others by giving them a clear understanding of the responsibilities of the job. Job responsibilities define the work people must do in order to achieve success. A manager has more power to achieve his own objectives when the people who work for him know what they must do to achieve success.

The Importance of Clearly Defining Responsibilities

The very first and perhaps the most important thing you can do to give people power is to tell them what they are supposed to do. There can be no success unless you clearly explain to people what is expected of them.

Sound simple? You say, of course your people know what their jobs are. They knew that before you hired them.

A reflection on your own career might cause you to ponder this issue a bit more carefully. How many times have you been caught in a trap because your understanding of what you were to do was different from your boss' understanding of it? Your sterling performance was all for naught simply because it was not the performance your boss was looking for. Or perhaps you got reprimanded for failing to do something simply because you didn't know it was your responsibility in the first place.

When people don't have a clear understanding of their responsibilities, confusion abounds. Time is wasted and energy is dissipated by anxiety and doubt. People spend much of their time second-guessing the boss, wondering if they are going in the right direction. Without a clear definition of their responsibilities, people are like ships at sea without compasses.

Will Initiative and Creativity Be Stifled?

Advocates of a laissez-faire style of management may argue that clearly defining responsibilities inhibits creativity and stifles initiative. By providing people with little or no direction, they believe they are fostering an entrepreneurial spirit. While this style of management may work in some situations, most people need boundaries and a very clear job description. Otherwise, they will fill in the gaps by inventing a job for themselves or modifying the job to suit their purposes.

Too little structure keeps people from using their power effectively. By having a clear definition of their responsibilities, people are able to focus all their energies on getting the job done instead of wondering what the job is, or working on the wrong activities. The more focused they are, the greater the power they have to achieve success.

Tell Them How Responsibilities Relate to Goals

It is not enough for people to know what they are to do; they must also know why they are doing it. They must be able to see the correlation between the responsibilities of their job and the goals and objectives of their department and the company. Otherwise the responsibilities they are asked to perform are nothing more than a list of meaningless activities.

Despite much talk today about the declining work ethic, most people want to be a part of something larger than themselves. The majority of people want to make a contribution; they want to make a difference. This desire, of course, may not be readily apparent. Having suffered at the hands of incompetent managers for years, many people eventually lose their desire, or at least it appears to be lost. The wise manager knows the desire is still there; it has just been lying dormant. His job is to rekindle it.

One of the tragedies in our complex American workplace is that many people don't have a sense of making a contribution. Most jobs are broken down into small parts and each part is given to a worker as his sole job.

The result is that many people have little or no idea what they are contributing to the end product and the whole social order. It is no wonder that many people work almost entirely for money but are unhappy no matter how much they receive.

If a person is to feel a sense of power and reach his poten-

tial, he must be motivated by something more than a paycheck. He must be able to see how his job, however large or small, contributes to the goals of the department, company, and society. A person must have sense of purpose if he is to have a sense of power.

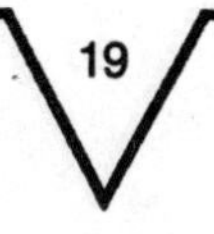

Communicate and Reinforce Responsibilities

Once you have clearly defined in your own mind the responsibilities of a particular job, the next step is communicating them to the person. Appears to be an easy task. Right? Tell the person once when he is hired and there should be no problem. Right? Wrong. People must be told not once, not twice, but repeatedly.

If a person is conscientious and capable of performing the job, why must you remind him of his responsibilities? If he has to be told more than once, maybe he doesn't belong in the position.

Reminding people of their responsibilities is similar to reminding them of the goals and objectives. Due to the complexity of jobs and companies today, people on all levels can easily become sidetracked.

It's not unusual to see people, even at high levels, involved in activities that are not in fulfillment of their job responsibilities. Nor do these activities contribute to the goals and objectives of the department or company. This is one of the primary reasons why companies don't reach their objectives: People concentrate their efforts on activities that seem like good ideas at the time but that don't lead them to their desired objectives.

People also have a natural tendency to do the things they like to do. They gravitate to certain types of activities because they are good at them and enjoy them. The result? The responsibilities they don't enjoy go unfulfilled because the people either consciously or unconsciously let them fall through the cracks.

When to Communicate and Reinforce Responsibilities

How do we communicate responsibilities to a person so that he has a clear understanding of what is expected of him? And how do we keep those responsibilities in the forefront of his mind so that he is always on track, working on the correct activities?

Before a person is hired he should be shown a written description of the job. At the time he is hired, he should be given a copy of the description to keep. When you review the responsibilities section with the person ask him for feedback. You want to make sure that his understanding of the responsibilities matches your own understanding.

The responsibilities section of the job description should be the basis upon which the employee's performance is evaluated. Therefore, it makes sense to review the responsibilities with the person at the beginning of each review period and at the time of the annual written review.

Whenever you verbally review the person's performance, which should be on a fairly frequent basis, the responsibilities should be reviewed at that time as well.

If you have difficulty with a person, if the person consistently works on activities that do not lead to the fulfillment of his or her responsibilities, you may have to review the responsibilities more frequently.

The objective is to make sure the person clearly understands what he is to do at all times. Understanding, of course, cannot take place without communication.

Distinguish Between Tasks and Responsibilities

Make sure people understand the difference between the responsibilities of their jobs and the tasks that must be performed in order to fulfill those responsibilities.

If a person receives a laundry list of tasks instead of a list of major responsibilities, he will have difficulty understanding how the job contributes to the accomplishment of the department and company goals. He may also restrict his activities to the list of tasks instead of the overall job to be accomplished.

A comprehensive list of responsibilities, as opposed to a detailed list of tasks, provides the person with a larger view of the job. It also gives people more freedom in deciding how to go about fulfilling the responsibilities of the job and meeting the established goals and objectives.

This is not to say that the manager shouldn't delegate tasks to the people who work for him. In some cases the manager should be quite specific as to what tasks should be performed in fulfilling the responsibilities. As a general rule, the more authority a person has and the greater the responsibility, the more freedom he should have in determining the tasks he will perform.

Building Pride Through Responsibility

If a person is to feel a sense of power in his job, he must feel a sense of pride—pride in the company, pride in the department or group, and perhaps most important, pride in himself.

Pride creates the desire to succeed; the desire to succeed causes people to dig down deep within themselves and draw upon untapped inner resources. Pride is perhaps the greatest catalyst for getting people to discover and use their own personal power.

One of the best ways to instill pride in people is by giving them a sense of responsibility; by helping them know that they have an important job to do.

A sense of ownership is what we are trying to create. This sense of ownership must be present if you wish to create an entrepreneurial spirit.

If a person believes the job is lowly and insignificant, if he believes that others look upon the job as relatively unimportant, his performance will usually reflect this belief. On the other hand, if you repeatedly remind him of the importance of his job, he will usually perform the job with a sense of pride and purpose.

Don't Duplicate Responsibilities

In order to create this sense of ownership and pride, a person must feel a sense of territorialism. Though territorialism can also be destructive, a certain amount of it is healthy and necessary. Nothing is more demoralizing to a person than to find that this very important job that has been assigned to him and him alone has also been assigned to someone else.

With responsibility goes authority. When you define job responsibilities to a person, make sure you haven't already delegated some of those responsibilities to someone else. Occasionally, there will be an overlap or duplication of responsibility between people in different departments. In this case, it is your job to resolve the conflict with your peer in the other department. Under no circumstances should the person working for you be left to battle that kind of problem on his own.

Prioritize Responsibilities

As we mentioned earlier, the job description is one of the tools you should use to communicate the job responsibilities. In addition to understanding the responsibilities of the job, a person must also understand the priorities of the job which are usually not reflected in the job description. The priorities of a job, of course, will change from time to time, depending upon the changing plans of the department and company.

Whenever the priorities change, review the changes with the person. All too often managers expect people to instinctively know when priorities change. Keep in mind that the people who are working under you are working with a different set of facts and information. They have a more limited view of what is happening within the company and the department. Therefore, they are not always equipped to make decisions regarding changes in their priorities.

Power comes from knowing what to do, knowing when to do it, and doing it in the correct sequence.

Inform the Team of Everyone's Responsibilities

Make sure the various members of the team understand one another's responsibilities. This is important, not just to the effective working of the individuals but to the effective working of the team. If the team is to have any power as a group, it must know who's on first, who's on second, etc. The power of an individual is decided to a great extent by the power of the group.

What to Do When Responsibilities Change

Remember that ego is always attached to responsibilities and when the responsibilities assigned to a person change, the ego is affected. Regardless of why a change was made, people will usually assume that the change is an indication of how pleased the manager is with their performance, which may or may not be the case.

A person should always have a clear understanding of why his responsibilities have changed. Otherwise, he will invent his own reasons which may adversely affect his morale and self-esteem.

If a person is, in fact, given greater responsibility because he has performed well, he should be told just that. On the other hand, if his responsibilities are changing because he has not performed up to standard, he should know that too. In the first case you can use this as an opportunity to build pride and motivate the person to greater achievements. In the latter, you can use it as an opportunity to help the person understand his weaknesses and where he needs to improve.

The decision to increase or take away a person's responsibilities should not be based solely on the individual's performance. The primary consideration should be the work to be done and how that work can be accomplished most effectively. When a person's responsibilities are changed he should understand the business considerations as well.

Summary

In order for a person to experience a sense of power in the job, he must have a clear understanding of the responsibilities of the job. Here are some things to keep in mind as you assign and communicate job responsibilities to the people who work for you.

- Clearly define the responsibilities of the job.
- Give people a sense of purpose by showing them how their job responsibilities relate to the department goals and objectives.
- Communicate and reinforce the responsibilities on a regular basis.
- Distinguish between responsibilities and tasks.
- Help people feel a sense of pride and ownership in the responsibilities that have been assigned to them.
- Avoid duplication of responsibilities.
- Prioritize responsibilities as plans change.
- Help team members understand one another's responsibilities.
- Communicate changes in responsibilities in a way that builds morale and/or helps people grow.

When you communicate job responsibilities in these ways, a person will not only have a better understanding of what is expected of him, he will also have a greater sense of purpose and pride—all of which are essential to feeling a sense of power.

The benefits to the manager are manifold. The time he spends performing these activities will pay big dividends. There will be greater efficiency because people will be working on the right activities. There will be greater productivity because people will be more motivated, and the quality of the work will be higher because people will have more pride. The end result? More power for the manager.

CHAPTER

2

POWER THROUGH AUTHORITY

Power Principle: A manager empowers others by giving them authority equal to the responsibility assigned to them. People can fulfill the responsibilities of their jobs only to the extent that they have been given the authority to do so. A manager has more power to achieve his own objectives when the people who work for him have the authority to fulfill their responsibilities.

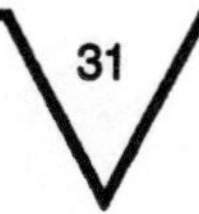

Importance of Delegating Authority

Most people equate authority with power. They constantly strive to increase their authority, believing that it is the beginning and end of their power. It is a day of grave disillusionment for most people when they arrive at a place of high authority only to find that they are still unable to get the job done. Authority is only one piece of the power picture. Nevertheless, it is a very important piece. Without authority, a person is powerless in his ability to get the job done and achieve success.

One of the most common complaints heard in the workplace today from people at all levels is "I have the responsibility but I don't have the authority to get the job done." This is one of the primary causes of stress in the workplace.

Nothing can compensate for a lack of authority. Not skill. Not desire. Not intelligence. Nothing. A person is severely limited in his ability to use his talents and abilities for the benefit of the company if he doesn't have the authority to put them into action. He will eventually lose his desire to use his talents if he is repeatedly blocked in his efforts to achieve success because of a lack of authority.

How Much Authority Should You Delegate?

Authority, like power, is hoarded in most companies. Managers delegate authority with great trepidation, which is one of the reasons why there is so much bureaucracy in large companies. There is always the possibility that a person will abuse the authority that has been given to him. In most cases, however, it is better to err on the side of giving a person too much authority rather than too little. When people have authority they tend to take more initiative.

So how much authority should you give an employee? Enough to fulfill the responsibilities that have been delegated to him. If a person is to be held responsible for the results he achieves, he must have the right to make decisions within the limits of his responsibilities.

What happens when a person is given too little authority? The amount of responsibility he is able to fulfill will shrink to the level of the authority. When a manager fails to delegate authority, the responsibility and therefore the work stay with the manager. In theory, the unfilled responsibility stays with the manager. In reality, however, what often happens is that the person is reprimanded for not completing the job. The manager is the one at fault for not having delegated the proper authority but his employee is the one who takes the rap.

In determining how much authority to give to a person you should first look at the job to be performed. Ask yourself how much authority will be needed to fulfill those responsibilities. At this point you are looking at authority solely from the perspective of the work to be accomplished.

After you have examined the job you'll want to take the

person into consideration. How capable is the person of exercising the authority assigned to the job? Depending upon your answer, you may want to modify the authority level somewhat. Let's say, for example, that a person is new to a job. He may not be equipped to fulfill all of the responsibilities and exercise all of the authority assigned to the job immediately. For a period of time you may ask him to consult with you on certain decisions until he gets up to speed.

Or let's say that you have an employee who has been working in the same job for a fairly long period of time. He has mastered the job and is performing above standard. In addition to performing his current job, he is preparing for his next position. In this case you may want to give the person authority greater than that which is assigned to the job.

The point we are making is that the authority assigned to the job should always be equal to the responsibility. From time to time, however, it may be appropriate to give a person a little more or a little less authority depending upon where he is in terms of being able to meet the job standard.

Communicating Authority

A person must have a clear understanding of his authority; otherwise he will spend much of his time walking on eggshells. People who walk on eggshells rarely achieve their objectives. They live in constant fear of overstepping their bounds or being reprimanded for leaving something undone. Their personal power is all but extinguished by their fear of failure.

People are often confused about how much authority they have because managers assume that they automatically know their authority levels. Some managers confuse responsibility with authority. They believe that authority is implied in the responsibility—whatever a person has to do to get the job done, that's what he should do. This, of course, is a sure way to get everyone in trouble!

Before a person is hired he should be told how much authority he will have in the job. For most people, particularly those in higher-level positions, the amount of authority they will be permitted to exercise is a major consideration in whether or not they will accept the position. Be as clear as possible on this issue during the interview process. Many a person has been disillusioned in a new job upon discovering that his actual authority is much less than what he thought it was going to be.

After the person is hired you will, of course, want to review the written job description. As you review the responsibilities, you should review the corresponding authority levels.

The job description usually defines the authority assigned to a job in very broad terms. You may want to give the person a more detailed description of his authority, depending upon the job. For example, if you are hiring a manager you will want to tell him what kinds of authority he has in terms of hiring and firing employees, which may not be described in the job description.

As you delegate major tasks to the people who work for you, from time to time you may need to clarify the boundaries of their authority. In some situations, you may want to give them more or less authority than usual, depending upon the task and the people involved. At all times, of course, the authority should be equal to the responsibility.

As well as to the person in the job, the authority assigned to the job should be communicated to the people with whom he will be working. When people don't have an understanding of one another's authority levels, problems are inevitable. In order for a person to effectively exercise power over others, people must believe that the one exercising the power has officially been granted the right to do so.

Authority As a Means to Growth

Authority provides a person with the official right to make decisions. Without decision making there can be no growth on the part of the individual or the company. When a person makes a decision he must use his mind to think and analyze; otherwise he operates by rote. If a person operates by rote long enough, eventually he forgets how to think and use his mind constructively. It is only by exercising the powers of one's mind that a person is able to move on to higher levels of achievement.

Most companies that grow successfully over time provide their people with plenty of authority all the way through the ranks. They recognize that the company's growth is inextricably linked to each individual's growth. They also realize that the company's growth is contingent upon its ability to make sound business decisions on a timely basis. Growth is impossible when all the decisions are made at the top.

Building Pride Through Authority

Since most people equate authority with power and power with importance, when you delegate authority you should use it as an opportunity to build pride and self-esteem. Authority should be earned, not increased indiscriminately. When communicated to a person in this way, authority is seen as a reward for past performance.

A person's authority defines his territory. Earlier we talked about the importance of helping people feel a sense of ownership and pride in the job; that a certain amount of territorialism is necessary if there is to be any kind of entrepreneurial spirit. A person cannot feel a sense of power and ownership if he doesn't know the boundaries of his territory.

We are back to the issue of ego. Few things make us feel more important than authority. When we feel important, we believe we can achieve. When we believe we can do something, we are halfway there.

How to Delegate Authority Without Losing Control of the Work

The number one reason why managers fail to delegate authority is because they are afraid of losing control. To lose control is to lose power. Some managers do in fact lose control when they delegate authority, not because they have to but because they fail to follow up. They get burned by their own hand and then decide to play it safe by keeping their authority to themselves.

Delegation of authority and control must always go hand in hand. Whenever authority is delegated there is some risk involved. A manager minimizes those risks by establishing the necessary controls—by following up periodically to see how well the person is exercising the authority that has been delegated to him.

When managers and companies don't achieve their objectives, very often it is because there is a lack of control and follow-up. The best-laid plan is useless unless there is some kind of system for monitoring how people are following the plan. Included in the plan should be a description of who has the responsibility and authority to do what.

If you are one of those who prefers to play it safe by delegating as little authority as possible, be forewarned. Sooner or later it will catch up with you. This is especially true if your responsibility grows. The greater the responsibility you have, the greater the need you have to let go of some of your authority. Otherwise you will be choked by the bottleneck that you yourself have created.

There is a remedy for the anxiety that comes with letting go of authority. Whenever you delegate authority you should also have a plan for following up to see how well the person is performing. Here are some ways you can keep tabs on how well a person is exercising his authority:

- Schedule regular counseling sessions with the person.
- Require the person to submit weekly and/or monthly status reports.
- Hold regular staff meetings.
- Obtain feedback from others.
- Spot-check the person's work.
- Implement quality-control procedures.

Minimizing Conflicts over Authority

Conflicts over authority are inevitable. As people battle over territory, they will battle over who has how much authority over whom. It is a problem that is unavoidable; however, there are things that can be done to minimize the severity of the problem. Here are some guidelines for avoiding conflicts over authority:

- When assigning authority to a job, make sure the authority does not inappropriately usurp the authority of other jobs in the department or in other areas within the company.
- Make sure the person clearly understands the authority that has been assigned to him.
- Make sure that everyone concerned with the person understands the authority assigned to him.
- Establish a system of controls for ensuring that the person is exercising his authority correctly.

Reassessing Authority Levels

Authority levels should never be engraved in stone. They must be adjusted from time to time to meet the changing needs of the business and the changing responsibilities of the jobs. Assigning the appropriate authority levels to jobs at all levels is critical to the efficient operation of any business, particularly those businesses that offer a service. One of the primary causes of consumer discontent stems from people not having sufficient authority; the customer is bounced around hither and yon before he finally reaches a person who is able to make a decision concerning his problem.

Here are some questions to ask yourself as you periodically reassess the authority levels assigned to jobs in your area:

- Have the responsibilities of the jobs changed in any way?
- If the responsibilities have changed, how should the authority levels be changed?
- Do the authority levels enable the company to meet its clients' and customers' needs as efficiently and effectively as possible?

This reassessment of authority levels is especially important to maintaining employee morale. If a person is given an increase in responsibility without a corresponding increase in authority, the result can be as devastating as failing to give him an increase in salary.

What to Do If a Person Abuses Authority

There will always be those who will abuse the authority that has been delegated to them. They may use it to intimidate and steamroll over others or they may simply overstep the boundaries of their authority by making decisions that are not theirs to make. Whenever this happens you should take immediate action. Unbridled authority can have a damaging effect on all concerned, including the person who is abusing the authority. Here are some suggestions for what to do:

- Gather all the facts regarding the situation.
- Meet with the person who abused the authority to discuss the problem.
- Review the boundaries of his authority and how he was in error.
- Try to find out why he abused his authority.
- Explain how his behavior is damaging to himself, other people, and the company.
- Try to get the person to agree that he will do differently in the future.
- Follow up in the future to see if the person has in fact corrected his behavior.

Some people have great difficulty with authority figures and consequently have difficulty exercising authority themselves. If a person repeatedly abuses the authority that has been granted to him, you may need to take away some of his authority for a period of time until he can learn to exercise it in a responsible manner. If that doesn't work, you may need to find another person for the job.

Summary

Authority is one of the cornerstones of power. Here are some guidelines for delegating authority that will help you empower the people who work for you:

- Always delegate authority equal to the responsibility.
- Consider the competence of the person when delegating authority.
- Tell the person before he is hired how much authority he will have.
- When the person is hired, review the responsibilities of the job and the corresponding authority levels.
- If the job description doesn't adequately define the authority levels, give the person a more detailed description.
- When delegating large tasks, be sure to clarify the boundaries of the person's authority.
- Communicate the person's authority levels to the people he will be working with as well as to the person himself.
- Use authority as a means to help the person grow.
- When increasing authority, build pride by explaining that the authority granted is a reward for past performance.
- Establish controls to ensure that the person is exercising his authority properly.
- Reassess authority levels from time to time.

- Watch for and resolve conflicts of authority.
- If a person abuses his authority, take the necessary corrective action.

A person's ability to achieve success hinges on his ability to make decisions. When he has authority equal to his responsibility, he is free to make the decisions and take the actions necessary to achieve his objectives.

Authority is also a great motivator because it is a symbol of trust. When people feel trusted, they are more likely to give the job their best effort.

When people have the authority to do the job on their own without constantly having to go to the manager, the manager is able to make better use of his time. He is able to devote his energies to more important activities—activities that will lead him to success.

By delegating the proper authority the manager is also free of the morale problems that result when people don't have the necessary authority.

CHAPTER

3

POWER THROUGH STANDARDS OF EXCELLENCE

Power Principle: A manager empowers others by setting standards of excellence that enable them to reach their full potential. When asked to stretch beyond their self-imposed limits, people discover powers they never knew they had. A manager has more power to achieve his own objectives when the people who work for him work to their full capacity.

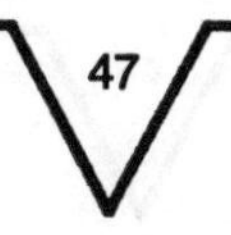

Importance of Setting Standards of Excellence

This chapter is for the reader who thinks the ideas in this book border on mollycoddling. It is for the reader who fears that he will overindulge and spoil his people if he spends too much time satisfying their needs.

Some managers think that if you are too nice to people they will become soft and lazy. First, we must define what we mean by "being nice to people." It doesn't mean letting them do whatever they wish. It doesn't mean letting them off the hook easily when they have missed the mark. And it doesn't mean giving them perks and special privileges.

The nicest thing you can do for the people who work for you is to empower them by applying the ideas in this book. Yes, you will satisfy them in the process but not at the expense of the company. The satisfaction of your people and the satisfaction or success of the company are not mutually exclusive. Each is dependent on the other.

So how does this relate to the issue of standards of excellence? The point is that when you treat people with respect, when you strive to meet their needs, you earn the right to demand superior performance. You create the kind of environment where they are able to meet standards of excellence. Furthermore, if you meet the needs of your people, they will naturally want to meet the high standards you have set for them.

It is impossible to build pride unless you set high standards. When people achieve excellence they not only distinguish themselves in the eyes of others, they experience the indescribable feeling that comes from having achieved the extraordinary. They feel like winners. Unfortunately, all too many people in today's workplace are robbed of this experience. No one challenges them or requires that they do anything other than mediocre work.

Once people experience the thrill of achievement, however, they are never quite the same. The word "work" suddenly takes on a new meaning. They have a newfound respect for themselves. They want to experience the "high" that comes from doing superior work, again and again.

One of the best-kept secrets in corporate America today is that people are aching to be "turned on" by their work. The way to turn people on is to ask them to work and stretch more than ever before and then let them experience the ecstasy* that comes from having given it one's all, from being the best at something, whether it is organizing files or closing the big deal.

If managers across the country would give people this experience, a new work force would be born and productivity would explode. The masses of apathetic, comatose-looking people who are currently marking time in their jobs would be transformed into an army of motivated people capable of far more than anyone ever dreamed possible.

*The word "ecstasy" may seem inappropriate when used in the context of job performance. It is possible, however, to give people this experience. A case in point is the Bowery Savings Bank in New York during the early 1980s. Faced with high teller turnover, management radically changed the image of the teller position. Tellers received extensive training and were required to pass the final exam with a score of 100 percent. The results? Turnover dropped to less than 5 percent and tellers experienced a remarkable sense of pride and accomplishment that was nothing short of ecstasy.

Setting Standards—Not Too Low, Not Too High

Having standards is not enough. They must be the correct standards. By correct we mean not too low, not too high. If you set them too low you will lose productivity; valuable resources will be wasted. Low standards are also demotivating. Challenge and job satisfaction go hand in hand. When standards are too low people become sloppy in their work. When they can do their jobs with their eyes closed, their attention is lost and needless errors are made.

Standards that are too high are a problem as well. When standards are unrealistically high, the manager has no yardstick for determining how well the people performed. The standard is meaningless.

Standards that are too high are also demotivating. If people know that the standards are impossible, they will reason "Why try at all? We can't reach them anyway." The standards become a source of frustration. If people consistently strive to meet the standards without success, they will feel like failures which will eventually affect their morale and performance.

The goal is to set standards high enough so that people have to work exceptionally hard to reach them and low enough so that they are attainable.

How and Where to Set Standards

For our purposes here, we will define a standard as a criterion for measuring performance. All standards fall into one of four categories. In other words, there are four ways to measure performance:

1. The quantity of the work to be done
2. The quality of the work—or how it is to be done
3. The cost of doing the work
4. The time it will take to do the work

In any business, these four factors constitute the basis for managerial control. Your job as a manager is to establish standards for quantity, quality, cost, and time for each major work activity in your area. It is also your job to find ways to increase quantity and quality and decrease cost and time.

Standards for quantity, quality, cost, and time should actually be established on three levels—the company, the department, and the job.

Company-wide standards are standards that everyone in the company is expected to meet. They are established by top management and should reflect the company's values and philosophies. These standards may include things such as how the telephone is to be answered, how people are expected to dress, and how customers and clients are to be treated.

Department standards are usually set by the department heads and should be consistent with the company-wide standards. These are expectations that are specific to the work of a particular department. These standards may include things such as the formatting of reports, cooperating with other members of the department, attendance, and punctuality.

And last, standards should be established for each job. These standards should be consistent with the department and company standards. If the job is one that is held by many people, for example, the position of bank teller, the standards may be set by someone other than the immediate manager. Job-specific standards may include standards such as the number of widgets to be produced, the amount of time to complete a job, and the number of sales calls to be made.

All the standards that are set within a company, regardless of where they are set, should reinforce the company's overall standard of excellence.

Communicating and Reinforcing Standards

You cannot expect a person to meet the standard if he doesn't know what the standard is. Sounds obvious, doesn't it? Unfortunately, it is the obvious that managers most often forget to apply.

Sometimes managers get so caught up in telling a person what to do that they forget to tell him how to do it. The manager has very clear expectations in his own mind and assumes that the person naturally knows what those expectations are.

People should be encouraged and expected to ask for clarification when they don't understand what is expected of them. Nevertheless, it is the manager's responsibility to communicate the standards and ensure that understanding has taken place.

Like goals and responsibilities, standards should be communicated over and over again. Since the company standards reflect the values and philosophies of the company, they should always be communicated during the interview process. The interview is a person's first impression of the company. From the very beginning, the person should understand that this is a company that has very high standards of performance—standards that everyone is expected to meet.

On the first day of the person's employment he should be given a written copy of all the standards—company, department, and job. During the orientation process, one of the central themes should be the importance of meeting standards of excellence.

The standards are the basis upon which a person's performance should be evaluated, so whenever you review performance, you should begin by reviewing the job standards. This way they will know what they are being evaluated against.

Standards should be reinforced on an ongoing basis. Staff meetings are an excellent time to remind people of the company and department standards. It is also a good time to compliment people for having achieved the standards. In addition to reinforcing the specific standards, you should constantly make reference to the importance of striving for excellence. The standard of excellence should be the umbrella under which all the other standards fall.

Motivating People to Achieve Excellence

Getting people to achieve excellence is no easy task. This is particularly true if the people you are managing are accustomed to doing mediocre work. They are perfectly happy, or at least they think they are, going about their humdrum way, doing average work. There's no strain, no push, no stretch. Then along comes a manager who expects double the effort, three times the output, and vast improvements in quality. Talk about rebellion. The people are incensed that this new chief would dare to upset their work group which in their eyes has been functioning perfectly well for quite some time.

People simply don't like to change and they will fight it every step of the way. When people have to stretch and do things they aren't accustomed to doing, it hurts. They have to use muscles, primarily the ones in their cerebral cortexes, that they haven't used in a long time, if ever.

In many cases people won't believe that the standards you have set are even attainable. Or if they are attainable, people will think it is inhuman to ask anyone to try to meet them. They will probably accuse you of being cruel and insensitive.

When you get this reaction, remind yourself that it is perfectly normal. It's part of the process. Provided your standards are high but realistic, it will simply be a matter of time before they are able to achieve what they presently think is impossible. Or should we say a matter of time, patience, and work on your part.

Don't expect people to go from mediocrity to excellence overnight. And don't be too concerned if they are not looking forward to the thrill of doing great work. Remember, many of them don't know what the experience is like, so you cannot expect them to be enthused.

Your job is to bring them step by step, almost imperceptibly, to the point where they can meet the standards and take pride in doing so. You will know you have arrived when the people reporting to you begin to enforce the same high standards on the people who work for them. When they become frustrated and amazed when the people who work for them don't meet the very standards that six months before they thought were so unfair, you have done the job. That's the point at which it has become their standard instead of yours.

This is critical to the issue of power. In order for a person to have a sense of power he must be motivated from within. He must be motivated to perform superior work for reasons other than the fact that he might be reprimanded by his boss or lose his job if he doesn't meet them.

Your job is to make excellence the norm rather than the exception. You want to create the kind of work group where the members of the group put pressure on one another to meet the standards. There is more power in peer pressure than any pressure that you yourself could bring to bear.

Getting people committed to excellence is difficult because you are asking them to radically change the way they think about themselves and their work. You're asking them to change their behavior. Depending upon the ages of the people and their prior experience, you will have to spend a lot of time and effort reversing ingrained patterns of thinking. But it can be done, if you are willing to do the work. Here are some things you can do that will help you get people to buy into excellence:

- When you tell them the standards, let them know what the rewards will be for reaching them.

- Compliment people in front of their peers when they meet the standards.
- Make sure they receive the training they need to meet the standards.
- Constantly remind people of the contribution they are making to the department and the company.
- Promote the achievements of your people to other people within the company via the employee newsletter, memos, etc.
- Acknowledge any hardships they may be having reaching the standards. Give them constant encouragement.
- Be patient with their moaning and groaning until their "muscles get stronger," until they experience the rewards that come from having achieved excellence.
- Let people know that it is through performance not politics that they will move ahead.
- Don't give up on them. The kind of change you are looking for takes a long time.

Setting the Example

One of the best ways to get people to achieve excellence is to inspire them through your own example. No matter how much you talk or what you do, if you aren't stretching and growing, if you aren't giving until it hurts, forget about asking them to do so.

Most Olympic athletes got to where they are because they were inspired by an Olympic athlete who preceded them. Few of us, if any, have the capacity to be self-inspired. We need another person to help light the flame.

You are their role model. How your people perform will always reflect to some degree the behavior and ideals you live out on a day-to-day basis.

Virtually everything you do in some way implies a standard to your people—the way you dress, the way you interact with peers and superiors, whether or not you start your meetings on time, the quality of your work. It's a good idea to do a quick check on yourself from time to time to see if you are performing the way you want your people to perform.

What to Do When Standards Are Inconsistent

Sometimes within a company there is great inconsistency from department to department in terms of meeting standards. One department may consistently perform absolutely superior work while another botches virtually everything it touches.

This can make it extremely difficult for the manager who requires excellence. Nothing angers people more than to see another person doing half duty while they are giving the job everything they've got. The problem is compounded if the competent high performers in one department have to rely on the incompetent poor performers in another department.

Here are some suggestions for how to handle this type of situation:

- Encourage your people to keep the communication open with the people in other departments, no matter how incompetent they are. Discourage them from developing a "we-they" attitude.
- Constantly remind your people of the benefits they will receive from meeting high standards, regardless of what others may be doing.
- Explain to them that it takes time for people to change. (Hopefully, management is taking steps to correct the problem.)

- Encourage them to be role models for others.
- If your people are being hindered by the incompetence of others, try to work the problems out with your peer in the other department. If that doesn't work, communicate the problem to your boss.

Summary

In order for a person to discover his own personal power and reach his potential, he must be challenged to achieve standards of excellence. A person can never know what he is capable of until he stretches beyond what he has achieved in the past. Here are some guidelines for how you can get the people who work for you to meet standards of excellence:

- Make sure standards are high yet realistic.
- Set standards for quantity, quality, cost, and time for each job.
- Communicate and reinforce the company, department, and job standards on a regular basis.
- Motivate people to achieve excellence.
- Set the example by meeting high standards yourself.
- When other departments are negligent in meeting standards of excellence, take steps to minimize the adverse effects on your people.

When you give people the experience of achieving excellence you help them feel a greater sense of pride and self-confidence. You also enable them to grow and take on new challenges. Because they have more confidence and a greater ability to achieve, they have a greater sense of their own power.

When people are committed to excellence the manager has more power to achieve recognition and success. Ultimately, the manager will receive credit for the superior work performed by his people. When people are motivated to achieve excellence, the manager doesn't have to spend time correcting their work and doing the work for them. He is able to spend his time on activities that will lead him and the department to success.

CHAPTER 4

POWER THROUGH TRAINING AND DEVELOPMENT

Power Principle: A manager empowers others by providing them with the skill and confidence they need to meet the standards of excellence. People must be able to meet the standards if they are to have the power to achieve success. A manager has more power to achieve his own objectives when the people who work for him are able to meet the job standards.

So far we have discussed three ways a manager empowers the people who work for him. First the manager must give people a clear understanding of the responsibilities of the job. Then he must give them the authority to fulfill those responsibilities. And third, he must set and communicate standards of excellence that tell people how the job should be done. In order to meet those standards, people must be trained, which is the subject of this chapter.

The Importance of Training and Development

Your ability to succeed as a manager depends upon your ability to get work done through the people who report to you. If you expect quality work, you must train and develop your people. Otherwise, you will spend the majority of your time correcting errors, doing the work yourself, and dealing with their frustrations, not to mention your own.

Training is perhaps the most neglected of all the managerial functions and one of the most important. Many managers view training as a bothersome nuisance keeping them from their immediate goal, rather than a long-term solution to their problems. It's a nice thing to do when there is an occasional calm, but when the whirlwind starts, training stops.

Some managers try to take shortcuts. When asked why they don't train, they reply, "We don't have to because we hire people who already have the necessary skills and experience." While this may sound like a good alternative to training, in reality it doesn't work. There is no substitute for training. A person may have a wealth of skills and experience but he still must be trained in the ways of the company. He must understand the values and philosophy of the company, the company's policies and procedures, and the procedures that apply to the particular job. If a person doesn't receive this job-specific and company-specific training, he is limited in his ability to use his skills and experience effectively.

Other managers say they have no formal training program because their people learn on the job. They claim that experience is the best teacher. What they are forgetting is that it is also a very expensive teacher.

When people are forced to learn by trial and error, everyone suffers. The person feels like a failure through no fault of his own; the customer is frustrated by errors that could have been avoided; and the company loses money.

Training is also the pathway to growth. If people are to exceed the standards and move on to higher levels of responsibility, they must be trained. The growth of the company is dependent upon the growth of the people who make up the company. If the company expects to successfully take advantage of new opportunities, the individuals within the company must be constantly improving their skills and preparing themselves to take on greater challenges.

The wise manager knows that when he trains his people he is doing the single most important thing he can do to ensure his own success. By passing his knowledge and skill on to others, he is multiplying his own effectiveness by the number of people he trains. He is willing to make the short-term sacrifices in order to receive the long-term benefits.

Training and Self-Esteem

Training is one of the best ways to build confidence and self-esteem. Without self-esteem there can be no power. A person's ability to achieve success depends largely upon his belief in himself. When a person believes in himself, he is free to explore and develop his full potential. Unshackled by the chains of self-doubt, he discovers that there are no limits to what he can achieve.

When you give a person a new skill you increase his value to the company. You also enable him to satisfy more of his own needs. The old adage is true: "Give a person a fish and he can eat for a day. Teach a person how to fish and he can eat for a lifetime."

Training breeds independence. The more a person learns, the less he has to rely on the manager. Independence is the foundation of self-esteem.

The goal of every good manager should be to train his people so well that they eventually have little or no need for him. The consummate manager goes one step further. He teaches his people everything he knows even if it means that they will become so marketable that they are able to demand a higher-paying, more responsible position elsewhere.

Whose Job Is It Anyway?

If you are fortunate enough to work for a company that recognizes the value of training, it probably has a professional training and development department. In fact, this department may be so competent that you have decided to leave the job of training strictly to the pros. This way you can pay attention to the more important job at hand.

If this is your attitude toward training, a slight change in focus will help you look at the job of training a little differently. Think of your job as manager as enabling the people who work for you to get the job done instead of your doing the job yourself. If you think of your role as an enabler, training will naturally become a priority.

The success of all the training that takes place in a company rests with the manager. The manager must constantly reinforce what is taught in the classroom if the classroom training is to have any effect on the job. Most people don't learn and internalize information by hearing it only once. It must be drilled into them through constant use, repetition, and reinforcement.

Perhaps that is why so many managers think classroom training is a joke and a waste of time. When employees attend formalized training programs the company doesn't get its money's worth. There is no reinforcement on the job and the participants are not held accountable for learning and applying what was taught.

Training should be a philosophy that pervades the entire company. Every manager should first be a teacher. Before a manager can tell people what to do, he must first tell them how to do it.

Providing the Skill and the Will

All training, whether it is provided by the training department or by you, should accomplish two objectives. It should provide people with the skill, meaning the ability, to do the job. Or it should provide them with the will or the desire to do the job. Some training will accomplish both.

The skills training you provide your people will be dictated by the needs of the business and the current skills of the people. First, you must determine what your people need to learn. Here are some questions that will help lead you to the answer:

- What are the goals and objectives of the area?
- What are the responsibilities of each job?
- What are the standards the people are expected to meet?
- What are the skills needed to meet the standards, fulfill the responsibilities, and achieve the objectives?
- What are the current skills and abilities of the people?
- What is the deficit between the skills needed and the current skills of the people?

Providing people with the skills to do the job is only half the training job. People must be motivated to apply the skills they have learned; therefore, some of the training should be principally motivational in nature. As you develop a plan for motivating your people, you will want to ask yourself these questions:

- What should they know about the company in order to have a sense of pride (history of the company; the company's products and services and why they are superior; company achievements; traditions, philosophies, and values of the company)?
- What can I teach them about the department that will give them a sense of pride (department accomplishments, importance of the department to the company, reputation of the department in the eyes of others)?
- What kinds of personal growth training will enhance their self-confidence and personal pride (training on how to present a professional image, interpersonal skills training)?

Training Methods

When we think of training we usually think of it in the formal sense. As you develop your training plan, keep in mind that training can take many different forms. The more varied the training, the better. Here are five ways you can provide your people with the skill and the will to do the job.

Formalized Classroom Training

This type of training is usually provided by the training department. It is your responsibility to let the training department know what kinds of training your people need. The training department is there to serve you but it cannot serve you effectively unless you communicate your needs to it.

If the training department is providing technical training for your people, you should provide input into the course development. You may be asked to provide technical consultants who will assist in the development of the program and perhaps even teach the program.

Don't place too many expectations on the classroom training. If you hope to get any benefit from it, you will want to develop a plan for reinforcing what was taught in the classroom on the job.

On-the-Job Training

The on-the-job training should make the classroom training come to life. The classroom training provides a totally controlled environment while the on-the-job training provides a semicontrolled environment. The idea is to gradually ease people into their jobs until they can perform the jobs on their own with relatively few errors.

It isn't necessary to do all the on-the-job training yourself. You may want to appoint a member of your staff to serve as an on-the-job trainer. If you do, make sure you select the right person. He should be respected by his peers. He should also have the ability to teach and communicate effectively. Just because someone has the necessary technical skills doesn't mean he has the skill to transfer his technical skill and understanding to others.

Here's one more way you can use the training department as a resource. Ask it to teach your technical experts how to train on the job.

Staff Meetings

Staff meetings are one of the best forums for training. Every staff meeting is an opportunity to instill pride in people by providing them with information about the company and the department. It is also a good time to train people on departmental policies and procedures.

One-on-One Counseling

Much of the training you provide your people should take the form of one-on-one counseling. In fact, the primary objective of every counseling session should be learning, not simply reprimanding and correcting performance.

Your Own Example

Remember, your people are constantly watching you. As they watch, they learn and emulate your behavior. So, make sure your example is a positive one. The best formalized training cannot offset the impact of a poor example.

Every good training plan includes a combination of at least these five methods and maybe others. By integrating all of them into one plan, you ensure that training is an ongoing process. When training is an ongoing process for everyone in the company, it becomes a powerful tool for change and growth.

How to Be an Effective Mentor

One of the buzzwords in management circles today is the word "mentor." It is one of those trendy words that actually has very old roots. What we know as a mentor relationship today is very similar to the old-time apprentice relationship.

A mentor is the ultimate trainer. He may be many things to his protégé, but he is first and foremost a teacher.

Sometimes managers are assigned the role of mentor, but in most cases a mentor relationship evolves naturally. For the person who is being "mentored," it can be one of the most significant relationships of his life. It can radically change the entire course of his career and open doors that can lead to success beyond his imagination. A true mentor is a catalyst for helping a person discover and make full use of his personal power.

An effective mentor relationship requires a significant investment of time and energy on the part of the manager. Because of the nature of the relationship and the time requirements, it is unrealistic to think that you can serve as a mentor for every person you manage. Here are some of the things you should consider in selecting a protégé:

- Potential. What kind of potential does the person have? What are his natural talents and abilities? What are the possibilities for the person in terms of career success?
- Character. What is the person made of? Does he have the character traits needed to fulfill his potential? Is he committed? Does he have perseverance and deter-

mination? Does he have a burning desire to succeed? Does he have integrity?

- Chemistry. Perhaps most important, what is the chemistry between the two of you? Is there a mutual admiration and respect? Do you share similar values? Do you like the person?

Mentor relationships are usually very special relationships. To some people, particularly those who have never participated in such a relationship, they are somewhat mysterious.

So how does one go about being a mentor to another person? If you are also the person's boss, in order to be a good mentor you must do everything described in this book, and then some. Here are some of the additional things you will want to do:

- Share your own personal experiences with the person.
- Share the wisdom you have gained through your own hard work and struggle.
- Help him create dreams for himself if he doesn't already have them. Work with him in developing career goals and a plan for accomplishing them.
- Help the person believe in his own potential through constant recognition and reinforcement. Pick him up when he falls down.
- Suggest learning opportunities outside the workplace.
- Help him broaden his view of the world and expand his vision.
- Constantly encourage him to go beyond his self-imposed limits. Give him challenges that slightly exceed his reach.

Your own greatest challenge in developing a mentor relationship with someone you manage will be maintaining that fine line of familiarity. If you become too close to the person, you may lose the person's respect. If you have to discipline the person you may find it difficult.

You also want to keep in mind the effect your relationship will have on the other people in your work group. You will have to work extra hard at not showing favoritsim and treating everyone fairly.

Summary

If a person is to have the power to achieve success, he must be trained to meet the job standards. Here are some things to keep in mind as you train and develop the people who work for you:

- Use training as a way to build self-esteem.
- Motivate people to learn by breaking down their resistance to change.
- Make training a priority.
- Work with the training department in developing an integrated training program that will meet the training needs of your people.
- Make sure that all the training provides people with the skill to do the job and/or the will to do the job.
- Make training an ongoing process by utilizing a combination of training methods.
- If you wish to serve as a mentor, make sure you select the appropriate person and do the things that make for a successful mentor relationship.

Training is one of the most important functions a manager performs. It provides a host of benefits: People are more confident, more knowledgeable, more competent, and more motivated. Consequently they make fewer errors and are more efficient and productive.

The manager has more power because he has a greater capacity to achieve the objectives of his area. People are able

to meet the job standards without his constant attention and guidance, so he is free to spend time on activities that will lead him to success. He has more power because he is able to multiply his own effectiveness by the number of people he trains.

CHAPTER

5

POWER THROUGH KNOWLEDGE AND INFORMATION

Power Principle: A manager empowers others by providing them with the knowledge and information they need to make good, sound business decisions. People must be able to make sound decisions if they are to achieve success. A manager has more power to achieve his own objectives when the people who work for him are able to make good decisions.

The Importance of Knowledge and Information

Expecting a person to perform a job without the proper knowledge and information is like asking a person to build a house without the necessary tools. It simply cannot be done.

A person may have a clear understanding of his responsibilities. He may have the necessary authority to fulfill those responsibilities. He may even have the skills and abilities to do the job. But if he doesn't have the necessary knowledge and information, he will be severely limited in his ability to fulfill those responsibilities, exercise his authority, and use those skills and abilities effectively.

Without the proper knowledge and information people are forced to operate in the dark. Lacking a firm foundation for making sound decisions, they make educated guesses instead and hope that they get lucky.

When people throughout the company make decisions in this fashion, the collective result is devastating. Disorganization and inefficiency are the hallmarks of a company that fails to give people the necessary information on a timely basis.

In Chapter 1 we mentioned that one of the reasons companies don't achieve their goals and objectives is because they work on the wrong activities. And why do they work on the wrong activities? Very often it is because they operate on incorrect and/or insufficient information.

Sometimes people are not even aware that they need certain information or that the information even exists. Here's where you as a manager are so important. You should con-

stantly encourage your people to seek out information on their own and at the same time anticipate the information they will need to do the job—information to which they may not have access.

Providing the necessary facts and information is critical to maintaining morale. Tell a person that his work is unacceptable because he was working with the wrong set of facts and you invite trouble. "Why didn't they tell us that in the first place?" is a question that echoes through the corridors of corporate America.

Pitfalls to Providing Knowledge and Information

Since we live in the Age of Information and have access to the most sophisticated information technology in the world, one would think that providing people with the proper information would be a cinch. Not so. Getting the right information to the right people at the right time is a major problem in most companies.

Some of the reasons have to do with the individual manager. Here are some of the more common reasons why managers fail to provide the people who work for them with the necessary information:

- The manager may fear that he will lose some of his power if he shares too much information. The insecure manager feels that he must "have something over" the people who work for him, and all too often that something is valuable information that the people need to do the job.
- Sometimes the manager simply forgets that his people need information or assumes incorrectly that they already have the information.
- The manager may have an inability to see how certain information is relevant to what another person is trying to accomplish. It is only after the fact that he realizes why a person needed the information.
- The manager may provide too much information and/or communicate it in a form that is difficult for people to understand and use. Overwhelmed by the

sheer volume or complexity of information, people fail to use any of it.

Other reasons for poor communications have to do with the company's communication system rather than the individual manager.

- The company may not have an effective system for tracking and communicating information.
- The organizational lines that should define the lines of communication may not be clear. Therefore, the flow of information is blocked.
- Managers of the various departments and divisions may not be held accountable for communicating information to other areas.
- Managers may have a lack of understanding of the company goals and objectives and the goals and objectives of other areas so they don't realize the need for communicating information to their peers.

It's a good idea to run through this list from time to time. It can be a useful tool for taking an inventory of how well you are providing information to the people who work for you. If you identify problems that have to do with the company-wide communications, you may want to suggest to your peers and to higher-ups that a task force be appointed to address the problem.

Determining How Much Information People Need

Some managers believe that the more they communicate to their people the better. While they are to be commended for their good intentions, they also need to be reminded of the problems created by providing people with too much information.

Time is a company's most valuable resource. It takes time to communicate and time to assimilate the communication. Here are some guidelines for determining whether information should be communicated:

- Is the information relevant to the person's job?
- Will the information help the person perform his job better?
- Does the person have the capacity to assimilate and utilize the information?
- Will the information help motivate the person by giving him a sense of purpose and pride?
- Is the information in a form that the person can easily grasp and use?

Knowledge and Information That Empowers

What kind of information should you give your people so they will have the power they need to do the job? Here is a partial list of information which should be given to every person within the company on an ongoing basis.

Company Goals and Objectives

Everyone within an organization, including those on the lowest level, should have some understanding of the company's goals and objectives. As we said in Chapter 1, goals and objectives are key to giving people a sense of pride and purpose. If communicated properly, the company goals can be a strong unifying force. They can be the glue that holds the team together. Unless there is a clear understanding of the company goals and objectives, there can be no teamwork. Without a common goal, people have no reason to come together in a spirit of cooperation.

Company and Department Plans

It's not enough for people to know the goals and objectives of the company and department. They must also know the plan. The goals are the destination. The plan is the path by which the team arrives at the destination. Giving people goals without giving them the plan is like telling them where

to go without telling them how to get there. There are usually a thousand and one ways to arrive at a single objective. Unless everyone is working from the same plan, chances are the team will never arrive. If the team doesn't arrive at its objectives, neither will the individual.

People are powerless in their ability to establish a sound realistic plan for themselves if they don't understand the plans of the company and department.

Information from Other Areas

There must be a sharing of information across departmental lines if the people in the various departments are to achieve their individual goals, the goals of their departments, and ultimately the goals of the company.

Everyone who works within a company either works in a line or a staff position. By line we mean those people who either produce the product or service, sell the product or service, or account for the company's finances. By staff we mean those people who support the people who work in the line. The staff people cannot support the people in the line unless they understand their objectives, plans, activities, and needs. Likewise, the people in the line cannot make good, sound decisions unless they receive the necessary information and support from the staff.

If a company is to achieve its objectives, it cannot function as a collection of independent entities working in isolation from one another. There must be a mutual sharing of information and a respect for one another's needs. The success of one department is dependent on the success of all the others. The power that an individual has to perform his job is dependent to a large degree on the information and support he is able to obtain from other areas.

Progress Updates

Tell your people from time to time how well they are doing in achieving the established goals and objectives. If you keep them in the dark regarding their progress, they may lose interest. They will reason, "Why stay on the road if we don't know how far we have come or how far we have to go?"

Progress updates are also a good way of keeping people focused on the goals and objectives.

Information About the Industry

One of the recurring themes of this book is the importance of giving people as broad a perspective as possible of what is happening within the company. If a person is to have a full understanding of the company's goals and objectives, he must also have an understanding of what is happening within the industry. Industry information provides a backdrop for company information. When people have an understanding of what is happening within the industry, they have a better understanding of the decisions made by executive management.

Information About Their Respective Discipline

People should also be kept abreast of changes and information relative to their particular discipline. For example, a person who is responsible for the data-processing function should stay up-to-date on technological advances. If the company is to remain competitive, people in the various areas of the company must be current on what is happening outside the company. Unless the company remains competitive, the

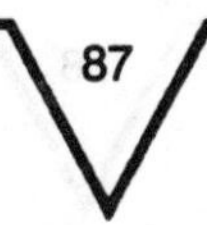

individuals within the company will be limited in their ability to achieve their own objectives.

Upcoming Changes

People naturally resist change. They usually reject change when it is forced upon them without prior notice. Communicating changes before they occur is important for two reasons: People have time to mentally adjust to the change and are more receptive to it, and people have time to incorporate the change into their existing plans.

As we mentioned previously, people should also be told the department goals and objectives and reasons for being proud of the company and the department.

Methods of Communicating

One of the definitions of communication is "the passing of information from one person to another with understanding." In order to achieve understanding it is important that we select the right method of communication. There are myriad ways to communicate. Here are some criteria for determining whether you are using the appropriate method:

- Will this method allow me to communicate the information on a timely basis?
- Is this the most cost-effective and time-efficient way to communicate?
- Do I need immediate feedback to ensure understanding, and if so does this method provide for it?

Here are two of the more common methods managers use to pass information on to others along with some guidelines for using them effectively.

Staff Meetings

Staff meetings are one of the best ways to communicate information to the people who work for you and they should be held on a regular basis. Staff meetings provide a host of opportunities. They enable you to motivate as you inform, encourage teamwork through the mutual sharing of information, and obtain immediate feedback on the information communicated. Here is a suggested agenda for regularly scheduled staff meetings:

- Update on company-wide news and events
- Reports by various members of the team on their individual activities
- Changes in company and/or department objectives and plans
- Activities of other areas that affect the work of the department
- Assignments and tasks to be performed
- Information needed from peers by individual members of the team
- Concerns and suggestions by team members as to how the department can function more effectively

In conducting staff meetings try not to dominate the discussion. Encourage participants to take an active role. Stick to the agenda and try to restrict the meeting to a specified length of time.

Memos/Reports

Memos and reports are perhaps the most commonly used medium for communicating business information and probably the most abused. The benefits of using memos and reports are that they allow the manager to communicate a lot of detailed information at one time. They also provide documentation of what was communicated that can be helpful in the future. The same message can be communicated to a number of people within a relatively short period of time.

The problem with memos is that they often go unread for one or more of the following reasons:

- They have no clear objective or purpose.
- They are too long.
- They are written in a way that is difficult for the reader to understand.
- Irrelevant data is included.

Reports are also a problem in many companies. Stacks and stacks of reports are generated and circulated on a regular basis and much of the time no one reads them because:

- The reports are sent to the wrong people.
- The reports are prepared in such a way that it is difficult to extrapolate the information needed.
- Too much information is communicated.
- The reports have not changed over time to meet the changing need of the managers.

If you are generating memos and reports within your area, you'll want to make sure that you are not guilty of any of these shortcomings. If your people are using memos and reports generated by other areas that are not meeting their information needs, you should work with your peers and/or higher-ups to make the necessary changes.

Summary

The age-old saying "Knowledge is power" is true and should be engraved in every manager's mind. Here are the things you should keep in mind as you provide people with knowledge and information:

- Don't guard and protect valuable information for fear that you will lose some of your power.
- Try to anticipate the information needs of the people who work for you.
- Encourage people to seek out information on their own.
- If there are company-wide communications problems that affect your people, try to work across organizational lines to correct them.
- Communicate only necessary information.
- Provide information on company and department goals and objectives, company and department plans, information from other areas, progress updates, information on the industry, information on the respective disciplines, upcoming changes, and reasons to be proud.
- Use the appropriate method for communicating.

When people have the necessary facts and information, they are able to make better decisions, faster decisions, and more decisions. They have more confidence in their decision-making ability because they have a basis upon which to make decisions. People are more motivated to make decisions because there is a greater probability that their decisions will be correct. Because they are able to make more and better decisions, they have more power to achieve success.

By providing people with the necessary facts and information, a manager is able to push decision making down to lower levels. The manager consequently has more power because he is able to devote his time and energies to more important activities and decisions. He doesn't have to spend endless hours making minor decisions and/or correcting mistakes that were made because people didn't have the necessary information. The productivity and efficiency of his area is higher because more people are making decisions and people are more motivated. Higher morale, higher productivity, and greater efficiency mean more power for the manager.

CHAPTER

6

POWER THROUGH FEEDBACK

Power Principle: A manager empowers others by giving them feedback on their performance. If people are to have the power to succeed they must know when and how they need to improve their performance. A manager has more power to achieve his own objectives when the people who work for him understand the changes they must make in their performance.

Importance of Feedback

People must receive feedback. Unless they know how well they are doing in fulfilling their responsibilities and meeting the standards, they cannot be expected to improve their performance when needed.

Many managers don't give feedback because they think people know without being told when they are doing a poor job or a good job. The manager who makes this assumption knows very little about human nature. Most people have a limited capacity to judge and evaluate their own performance and work. They need help in seeing their strengths and weaknesses. That goes for the excellent performer as well as for the poor performer.

People need to know when they are doing a superb job and when they need to improve and make changes. When they don't receive feedback, they become preoccupied with the question of how well they are doing. Are they going to get zapped or praised? Are they on the manager's good list or bad list? Are they going to get promoted or fired? These are difficult questions for anyone to live with.

When people don't receive the necessary feedback, they feel unnoticed, unappreciated, and uncertain. They usually find a way of getting some form of attention, usually negative, since that is the only thing some managers respond to.

It is impossible to establish an effective working relationship with people unless you give them feedback. There must be two-way communication if there is to be an understanding between you and the people you manage.

The Purpose of Feedback

Whenever you give feedback to a person on his performance, it should accomplish one or more of the following objectives:

- Reinforce positive performance
- Show the person how and where he needs to change and improve
- Motivate the person to perform better
- Build pride

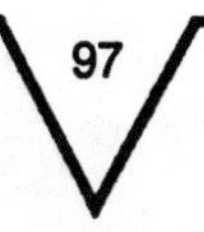

Ways to Give Feedback

There are a number of ways to give feedback. In order to accomplish your communications objectives, you will want to carefully choose the appropriate time, place, and method. Here are some of the ways you can give feedback to the people who work for you.

Counseling Sessions

Counseling sessions are one of the best ways to give people feedback and should be held on a fairly frequent basis. They should not be held solely for the purpose of reprimanding and correcting performance. In order for people to reach their full potential, they should be given three types of counseling:

1. On how well they have performed against the standards
2. On their strengths and weaknesses
3. On areas where they can develop beyond the current job

Performance Appraisals

Performance appraisals are one of the more formal ways of giving people feedback. Although the written performance appraisal is usually prepared only once during the year, a manager should appraise the performance and encourage the development of his people on a continuous basis. If a manager is doing his job correctly, the written performance appraisal should be a recap of all the counseling a person has received throughout the year.

Great care should be taken when you write and present a performance appraisal. The performance appraisal is a person's report card for an entire year's work. If you treat it as a bothersome administrative task deserving little of your time, you are doing your people a great injustice. They have a right to know how well they have performed and what they need to do in order to progress within the company.

Memos and Letters

When people have accomplished something extraordinary, put your praise in writing. Words are easy to say but it takes time and effort to write them down. Even if it is a two- or three-liner, people will appreciate it.

Letters on your personal stationary should be reserved for those special occasions when a person has worked exceptionally hard and has accomplished something truly outstanding.

Memos and letters can also be effective when a person has made a major error or has made the same error on numerous occasions. When you want a person to think long and hard about what he has done wrong, put it in writing. This should only be done on rare occasions.

There are two rules that should never be violated when giving people feedback via memos and letters:

1. Make sure the memo or letter is sent very close to the time of the event or accomplishment. A thank-

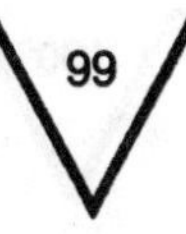

you note or a note of reprimand sent two to three weeks after the fact defeats the purpose of the memo in the first place. In either case, the memo or letter should be marked "Confidential."

2. Always personalize the memo or letter. If a group of people has worked exceptionally hard, don't send the individuals a memo addressed to the group. Sending an individual a memo addressed to the group is like throwing a crumb to a hungry person. When a person has given his all to a project he needs to be recognized as an individual, regardless of how many people were involved in making it happen.

Staff Meetings

Staff meetings provide an excellent forum for giving feedback to the group and individuals. Group feedback is especially important. People need to know how well the group as a whole is performing as well as how they are performing as individuals.

When you give feedback to the group, it can be either positive or negative. If you give feedback to an individual during a staff meeting, make sure it is positive.

Acknowledgment from Higher-Ups

Most of the feedback people receive should come from their manager. When they go far beyond the call of duty and accomplish something of great importance, arrange for feedback from someone higher up in the organization. Nothing makes people feel more important and appreciated than to be recognized by the "big boss."

Small Gestures

There are myriad ways to give people feedback. Some of the most meaningful ways can be the most simple—a handshake, a touch on the shoulder, a frown, a smile, a small token of appreciation. However you choose to give people feedback, make sure you plan it and think it through carefully. Make sure the form of feedback is appropriate for the occasion and the person.

Tailoring the Feedback to the Person

Feedback should always be tailored to the person you are addressing. Here's where understanding your people is so important. Whenever you give feedback to a person, you should take his needs and personality into consideration.

Feedback that is homogenized and the same for everyone is meaningless. If everyone who does an outstanding job gets the same slap on the back and the same "Good job," the feedback will be interpreted as insincere. Feedback must be personalized and sincere if it is to be effective.

Frequency of Feedback

Feedback should be given on a fairly frequent basis. Here are some general guidelines for when and how frequently to give feedback:

- Performance counseling at least once a quarter
- Written performance appraisal at least once a year
- Praise and reprimand as often as warranted
- Feedback at staff meetings at least twice per month

A word of caution. You can give too much feedback. If you comment on people's performance every time they make a move, the feedback will lose its impact. People will also feel as if they are under a microscope.

Feedback for the High Achiever

High achievers often get shortchanged when it comes to feedback. How many times have you heard a manager say, "He is the ideal employee. He does such a good job I rarely have to see him or talk to him"?

High achievers need and deserve just as much feedback as low achievers. The feedback will, of course, be of a different nature; nevertheless, it is just as important to the individual and the company. In both cases you are striving to maximize the potential of the person.

If you leave the high achiever on his own without guidance or feedback you are failing to develop and utilize your human resources. The low achiever may be given an opportunity to grow while the high achiever is deprived of the same opportunity. No matter how competent a person is, there is always room for growth and improvement.

Feedback for the Low Achiever

One of the primary reasons why many managers don't give feedback to their people is because they don't like the unpleasant job of telling people when they have done something wrong. What they are forgetting is that they are doing people a greater disservice by not telling them when they need to improve.

One of the saddest occurrences in the workplace today is the termination of people who have been with the company for a long time. The scenario is a common one. A person has been a loyal employee for twenty-five or thirty years. Times get tough, the company is taken over by new management, and the deadwood is eliminated.

The tragedy lies not in the fact that the long-term employees were terminated. Management had to do what was in the best interest of the company.

The tragedy lies in the fact that many of these people worked under the misconception for years that they were doing an excellent job. During the entire time of their employment, they received nothing but perfect reviews. No one ever suggested that they do things differently. Consequently, they had little power over their own destinies because no one had the courage to be honest with them.

Withholding information from people when they are not performing up to the standards is unfair. When it is withheld from a person over an entire career it is criminal.

When you do give feedback to low achievers, try to apply the positive approach whenever possible. The positive approach doesn't mean avoiding the issue or glossing over the need to improve. It means concentrating on how the job can be done better instead of what the person did wrong. It means providing the person with the direction and guidance he needs to meet the job standards. The positive approach keeps communication open; it does not put the person on the defensive.

The negative approach should be used only when all other means have failed. It should be used when you want to advise the person that he is on final notice.

Summary

People must be given feedback if they are to achieve their objectives and reach their full potentials. Here are some guidelines to keep in mind as you give feedback to the people who work for you:

- Counsel your people on a frequent basis.
- Give each person a written performance appraisal at least once a year. Make sure the written review is a summary of all the counseling you have given the person throughout the year.
- When you give feedback through memos and letters, make sure they are personalized and sent close to the time of the event or accomplishment.
- Always tailor the feedback to the person. Take the person's needs and personality into consideration.
- Use staff meetings as opportunities to give feedback to the group and individuals.
- When people go beyond the call of duty and accomplish something truly outstanding, arrange for acknowledgment from your boss or someone else higher up in the organization.
- Don't give too much feedback.
- Don't neglect the high achiever because he is able to meet the standards on his own. Provide him with feedback that will help him develop beyond the current job.

- Be honest with low achievers. Use the positive approach as much as possible.

Feedback provides people with power because it lets them know how well they are doing in achieving the objectives and meeting the standards. It lets them know when and how they need to change in order to achieve success.

Through feedback the manager is able to reinforce positive performancc, build pride and self-confidence, and motivate people to perform even better, whether they are low achievers or high achievers.

The manager has more power when he gives people feedback because there is better understanding and communication between him and the people he manages. Better communication and more motivated people provide the manager with power to accomplish the objectives of his area.

CHAPTER

7

POWER THROUGH RECOGNITION

Power Principle: A manager empowers others by giving them recognition which enhances their self-esteem and motivates them to continue to do their best work. A person's power to achieve success is dependent upon his belief in himself and his desire to do consistently excellent work. A manager has more power to achieve his own objectives when the people who work for him are confident and motivated to do their best work.

The Importance of Recognition

From the time we are born until the time we die we seek recognition. Within each of us is a driving need to know that we count for something; to know that we make a difference to at least one other person. Recognition is as necessary to the growth and well-being of a person as food and shelter.

Each of us brings to the workplace a multitude of needs, not the least of which is this need for recognition. As we have noted throughout this book, work has the capacity to fill many of our needs, provided we are fortunate enough to work for an enlightened manager. The enlightened manager knows that his own needs and the needs of the company cannot be met unless he meets the needs of the people who work for him. He also knows how to go about meeting those needs in ways that are mutually beneficial to all concerned.

One of the manager's primary jobs is to make people feel like winners. When people feel like winners they act like winners. It is a cycle that perpetuates itself. The person performs superior work. He is recognized for his accomplishment and made to feel important. He performs more good work in order to get further recognition and experience the same good feelings. When something feels good we naturally do whatever we have to do to experience that feeling again.

Recognition is important for another reason. It is information, a form of feedback. Unless you acknowledge a person's good performance he won't know to repeat the performance or behavior in the future.

Recognition As a Member of a Group

We all have a need to be recognized as individuals. We also have a need to be recognized as part of a group. Identification with a group enables us to satisfy some of our social needs. When the group we are associated with is a winning team, we get an added benefit. Through association with the group we feel like winners ourselves. Perhaps this is why people rally behind the home team when they are winning. By supporting the team, the fans are able to share in the glory.

Recognition of the group is important because it reinforces teamwork. A work group consisting only of "stars" usually doesn't function well. People must at times sacrifice some of their own needs in order to meet the needs of the group. By recognizing people as members of a group you let them know that teamwork is valued as much as "star performances."

Group recognition is important for another reason. Not everyone has the capacity to distinguish himself as winner individually. But everyone can distinguish himself by contributing to and being part of a winning team.

Recognition As an Individual

No matter how strong a person's identification is with the group or how proud he is to be a member of the group, he still needs to be recognized as an individual. When we recognize people as individuals we fill some of their psychological needs—we fill their need to stand out, to be someone important.

Ways to Recognize People

There are myriad ways to recognize people. The way in which we choose to recognize them sends messages beyond the mere content of the recognition—to both the person we are recognizing and to others. Here are some questions to ask yourself as you decide how to recognize a person for a job well done:

- Is the form of recognition appropriate for the achievement?
- Does the recognition convey sincere appreciation?
- Does the recognition fully acknowledge the person's accomplishment?
- Does the recognition acknowledge the person as well as the accomplishment? Does it reinforce the person's sense of self-esteem?
- How will the recognition be perceived by the person's peers? Is it equal to the recognition you have given to others for similar achievements?

Here are some of the ways you can recognize the people who work for you and some of the things you'll want to keep in mind.

Praise

Most people thrive on praise and can't get enough of it. Sometimes words are all we need. We simply need to hear how wonderful we are or see it in writing. When you recognize people through praise, choose your words very carefully. Make sure your words adequately reflect your true feelings and thoughts about the person's achievement.

Performance Appraisal

A performance appraisal is one of the best and most important ways to recognize a person. When you recognize people in this way you accomplish two objectives. You let the person know how you feel about him and you provide a permanent documentation of the recognition. The documentation will be important to the person's future growth and advancement within the company.

When you recognize a person through the performance appraisal, make sure you provide as complete a list as possible of his major accomplishments. As you note the accomplishments, be specific. A person who is unfamiliar with the work of the area should be able to read the appraisal and get a fairly complete picture of the person's accomplishments.

Promotions

Sometimes words are not enough. People need a larger demonstration of recognition. When people consistently grow and progress within a position, when they have mastered a job, they expect to be recognized through promotion to a higher position. Sometimes this is the only form of recognition that will satisfy a person.

When you recognize people through promotions, make sure the promotion is warranted. Don't promote a person to a higher position simply because you are afraid of losing him.

And don't promote people simply because they have served their time in the previous position. A promotion should always be recognition of a job well done and it should always be accompanied by a salary increase.

Increased Authority

One of the best ways to recognize people is to increase their authority when they have performed well and used wisely the authority they were originally given. When you expand a person's decision-making ability, in essence you are telling him that you are pleased with the decisions he has made in the past.

When you increase a person's authority make sure it is equal to the responsibility you have delegated to him. In other words, never increase authority merely as a means of recognizing a person for good work.

Monetary Recognition

When you recognize people in monetary ways, you put your money where your mouth is. As with promotions, there are times when this is the only type of recognition that will satisfy a person.

Raises and bonuses are two of the most meaningful ways of recognizing people, although many managers fail to fully utilize them as opportunities to build morale. When people receive standard raises and bonuses regardless of how they perform, the money no longer serves as a meaningful form of recognition. The raise or bonus becomes a routine, expected event rather than a meaningful response to performance.

Whenever you give a person a raise or bonus, make sure

you tie it to performance. Let the person know what he did to earn it.

Surprises and Special Liberties

Everyone likes a surprise. When you recognize people by surprising them with thoughtful, out-of-the-ordinary deeds, you communicate sincere appreciation. Your actions make the person feel special. Surprises can take any number of forms—tickets to a play, lunch with you, a bouquet of flowers—anything that shows thoughtful consideration and appreciation. Another way to recognize people is to let them take special privileges when deserved such as coming in late or going home early after working late the night before.

Working Side by Side with People

One of the best ways you can show appreciation to people who go beyond the call of duty is by rolling up your shirt sleeves and working alongside them. When you take time away from your own job to help the people who work for you, you give them one of the highest forms of recognition you can give. Your actions will speak louder than any words you can say.

Tailor Recognition to the Person

Recognition should always be tailored to the person. People have different needs; consequently they need to be recognized in different ways. Some, for example, will need more praise than others, depending upon their level of confidence and need for approval.

As you take the needs of your people into consideration, make sure you recognize them fairly and equally. Recognition should always be based upon what the person has done to earn the recognition rather than how you feel about the person. Be careful not to show favoritism.

Importance of Timeliness

When you recognize a person is as important as how you recognize him. People should be recognized as close to the time of the event or accomplishment as possible. Late recognition communicates a strong message to the person: "Your effort was not important enough to warrant my immediate attention." In order to reinforce good performance, recognition must be immediate.

Summary

Recognition provides people with the incentive to do superior work. Here are some guidelines to keep in mind as you recognize your people:

- Make people feel like winners.
- Recognize them as members of a group as well as individuals.
- Make sure the recognition is appropriate for the achievement.
- Give recognition in a way that conveys sincere appreciation.
- Be sure the recognition fully acknowledges the people's accomplishments.
- Recognize the people as well as the achievements.
- Make sure the recognition is equal to the recognition you have given others for similar achievements.
- Tailor recognition to the person.
- Make sure the recognition is timely.

When you recognize people for their performances you let them know how well they are doing in meeting the established standards. With this knowledge, they have greater power to achieve success. Recognition also empowers people by contributing to their sense of self-worth. It feeds their desire to achieve success.

When people feel good about themselves and feel appreciated, they are more motivated. Motivated people means greater productivity and efficiency which means power to the manager.

CHAPTER

8

POWER THROUGH TRUST

Power Principle: A manager empowers others by trusting in them, which helps them believe more in themselves. The more people believe in themselves, the more power they have to achieve success. A manager has more power to achieve his own objectives when the people who work for him believe in themselves.

In the preceding chapters we have discussed seven ways a manager can empower the people who work for him:

1. Provide them with a clear understanding of responsibilities.
2. Give them authority equal to their responsibilities.
3. Set and communicate standards of excellence.
4. Enable them to meet the job standards by training them.
5. Provide them with the knowledge and information they need to make good, sound decisions.
6. Give them feedback on their performances so they can make the necessary changes.
7. Recognize them for their efforts.

In order to fully empower the people who work for him, a manager must create a trusting environment, which is the subject of this chapter.

The Importance of Trust

Trust is vital to the health of any relationship. When you trust another person you enable him to feel safe and accepted.

This feeling of safety and acceptance must be present if people are to produce their best work. When people feel trusted they are free to concentrate all their efforts on the job, instead of worrying about how they are going to justify their actions. When they don't feel trusted, they live in constant fear of fulfilling your negative expectations.

Managers who are basically untrusting usually make snap judgments based on outward appearances. They don't take time to gather the facts and objectively evaluate situations. Consequently, the people who work for them spend enormous amounts of time and energy manipulating outward appearances, since that is all that matters. They constantly try to head off problems at the pass, problems that in many cases are nothing more than the manager's misperceptions.

When you trust another person you help to build his confidence and self-esteem. People who have low self-esteem usually don't trust themselves to do well. All too often their lack of self-trust is unfounded. Many people are capable and have good instincts, but because of prior conditioning they live in webs of self-doubt and anxiety.

Sometimes all it takes is the trust of another person for a person to learn to trust himself. The manager who says, "It's okay. I believe you can do it. I trust you." gives the person the courage and confidence he needs to take the risk. If this is done repeatedly for a person over time, he will eventually learn to trust himself. He will come to have a realistic view of his own talents and abilities.

Types of Trust

When we talk about trusting a person we are referring to two types of trust:

1. Trust in the person's character and integrity
2. Trust in the person's abilities

A person may be of the highest integrity but his abilities may not match his character. He may sincerely want to act in the best interest of the job and the company but he may not be able to because of some deficiency in his skills and abilities.

In other cases, a person may be fully capable of doing the job, but his motives and desires, which may be less than pure, will keep him from using his talents and abilities wisely.

Usually the former is easier to deal with. It is easier to give a person a new skill than it is to give him character.

Early on in a relationship and as the relationship progresses, you will have to determine how much you can trust the person. As you make this determination, be sure to address both criteria. Keep them separate in your mind so that you will have a realistic view of the person.

Blind Trust vs. Earned Trust

It is easy to say, "Trust the people who work for you." Oh, if it were only that simple. Unfortunately, we still have to deal with the reality that some people are not to be trusted.

We are not suggesting that you blindly trust everyone. Trust is something that must be earned by the people who work for you and they must understand that.

What is important is how you approach the issue of trust. Is your attitude one of "I will trust you until you prove to me that you are undeserving of my trust" or is it one of "I won't trust you until you prove to me that you are deserving of my trust"?

There are, of course, different levels of trust. Trust grows as people get to know one another better. In order for trust to grow, however, there must be a foundation upon which to build. This foundation is the belief that most people are basically good, that they genuinely want to do a good job. When you expect the best in a person you lay the groundwork for a trusting relationship.

Ways to Demonstrate Trust

There are a number of ways to let people know you trust them. How we feel about people and our actions will speak louder than any words we could say. Here are some of the ways you can show people that you trust them.

Delegate Important Tasks

The size and importance of the tasks you delegate to people will be a measure of the amount of trust you have in them. As a person proves that he is worthy of your trust, give him increasingly difficult tasks to perform. In addition to showing him that you trust him, you will also be helping the person to grow. Growth occurs best in a trusting environment.

Delegate Authority

As you delegate increasingly difficult tasks to people, you will want to increase their authority levels, which will be one more demonstration of trust. When you give a person authority, remind him that you are entrusting him with the company's welfare. Let him know that you trust his judgment and ability to make right decisions.

Give People Freedom

Don't hover over people. There is no better way to communicate distrust than by watching their every move. Assign the tasks, set the standards, ask for periodic updates on their progress, but beyond that, leave them alone.

Give People the Benefit of the Doubt

Always give people the benefit of the doubt. When you assume the best about people and situations, you'll be amazed at how many times you will find it. As hard as it may be, try to believe that they had a good reason for doing what they did, even when they have made a major blunder.

Allow People to Interface with Higher-Ups

Some managers keep their people hidden away from top management for fear they will say or do something stupid in the higher-ups' presence. Usually when a manager behaves in this way he is reflecting his own insecurities. The secure person takes the risk, knowing that his own good record will overshadow any minor mistake that his people might make. He recognizes how important it is for people to have this opportunity. If people are to grow in the job they must be able to relate to people at all levels within the organization.

When you let people relate to the "top brass," you give them one of the greatest votes of confidence you can give them.

What to Do When Trust Is Violated

When a person violates your trust, the first thing you want to do is ask yourself: "Did the person make an innocent mistake? Was it a question of a lack of skill and understanding or was it a question of wrong motives?" In order to arrive at the correct answer, you'll want to keep an open mind and be very objective as you gather your facts.

When It Is an Innocent Mistake

If you determine that the mistake was an innocent violation of trust, follow these steps:

- Explain to the person that he made a mistake.
- Ask the person why he performed in that particular way.
- Explain the results of the mistake.
- Let the person know how you feel about the mistake.
- Identify with the person how he should have done things differently.
- Let the person know that you believe he was well intentioned and that you're confident he will do better in the future.

When the Mistake Is Due to Wrong Motives

Mistakes that are made because of wrong motives are a bit more difficult to handle since the person's integrity is on the line. Here's how to handle this type of situation:

- Ask the person if he realizes he made a mistake.
- If he says he doesn't, explain to him where he was in error.
- Ask him why he performed as he did.
- Ask him if he understands the results of his mistake.
- If he doesn't, explain the results to him.
- Let him know how you feel about the mistake and that you expect him to do differently in the future.
- If the error is one he has made repeatedly, tell him what kind of action you will have to take if the problem continues.
- Let him know that you want to trust him but he will have to earn it back. Reaffirm his good points.

Summary

In order to get people to produce their best work, they must feel that you trust them. Here are some thoughts to keep in mind as you go about the business of trusting the people who work for you:

- Distinguish between trust in people's characters and trust in their abilities.
- Let people know that trust must be earned.
- Lay the foundation for trusting relationships by believing that people are basically good, that they genuinely want to do a good job.
- Remember that feelings and actions speak louder than words when you try to convey trust to other people.
- Demonstrate trust by delegating important tasks and corresponding authority.
- Give people freedom—don't hover over them.
- Give people the benefit of the doubt.
- Allow people to interface with higher-ups.
- When trust is violated, determine whether it was an innocent mistake or a mistake due to wrong motives, and then take the appropriate action.

When you trust other people you help them believe in themselves more. When people believe in themselves they have the power to reach their potential. When people feel trusted they usually repay trust with high performance.

The more motivated and productive people are, the more power the manager has to achieve his own objectives.

CHAPTER 9

POWER THROUGH PERMISSION TO FAIL

Power Principle: A manager empowers others by giving them permission to fail. When people are given permission to fail, they risk more and push the limits, which enables them to discover the full extent of their power. The manager has more power to achieve his own objectives when the people who work for him are able to utilize their imaginations and talents to the fullest.

The Importance of Letting People Fail

Throughout history the people who have achieved the greatest success in life have been those who were not afraid to fail. In fact, most of them failed time and again and often in a very big way.

Thomas Edison tried 2,500 times to invent the light bulb before he finally succeeded. Abraham Lincoln ran unsuccessfully for public office 6 times before he was elected president. History is replete with stories of famous people who were well acquainted with failure; people who set goals higher than what they at first could achieve and who then persevered until they became conquerors.

If a certain amount of failure is intrinsic to great success, why is it such an evil word? Why do most of us place severe limitations on ourselves in order to avoid failure, even to the point of sacrificing our dreams?

A person trained in the behavioral sciences could have a field day with this question. For our purposes here, in very simple terms, we can say that people are afraid of failure because they never learned to see it as a friend. Instead of seeing it as a stepping-stone to success, they view it as a blockade.

In order for people to realize their full potentials they must be given permission to fail. When this permission is granted, the element of fear is removed. Fear is the great enemy of power. As long as people are consumed by the fear of being rejected, the fear of losing face with their peers, or the fear of losing their job, they can never reach their full potentials.

When people are denied permission to fail, they play it

safe. Their reach never exceeds their grasp. They set goals lower than what they are capable of achieving. The result is that the company loses valuable productivity. Mediocrity instead of excellence is the norm. Business opportunities are missed. And the people are deprived of the exhilarating experience that comes from taking risks, beating the odds, and accomplishing the near impossible.

When to Let People Fail

There are some mistakes and failures that can, of course, be ghastly. We aren't suggesting that you encourage your people to take a devil-may-care attitude about their mistakes and failures. The idea is to free them of the fear of failure so that they can devote all their energies to the accomplishment of the objectives. When they fail you want them to see their failure as a learning experience rather than as a big black mark against their career.

In order for failure to be a positive experience for everyone, you must manage failure properly. Letting people fail anytime, anyplace is a sure way to commit career suicide. Here are some steps you can take in managing the failure of your people.

Help to Ensure Their Success

The best way to minimize the failures of your people is to apply the principles in this book. Tell them what their job is, give them the authority they need to do the job, set standards of excellence, train them, provide them with knowledge and information, give them feedback, recognize their efforts, trust them, and respect them. If you do this for each person who works for you, you will create an environment that is conducive to success.

Anticipate Failures

Always be on the lookout for potential failure. If you know your people well, you can almost predict when they are going to succeed and when they are going to fail. This doesn't mean that you have negative expectations of your people. It means that you have a realistic view of their capabilities.

When you anticipate failures they become less of a shock and you are able to plan for them. In some cases you will want to take steps to avoid the failure; in other cases you will want to let the person fail as a way of providing him with a valuable learning experience.

Weigh the Potential Cost of Failure

As you go about the process of determining when and how to let people fail, ask yourself these three questions:

1. What is the potential cost of the failure to the department and the company?
2. What is the potential cost of the failure to the person?
3. What is the potential cost of the failure to you, the manager?

In some cases the costs will be too high. If either the company, the person, or you will be severely hurt by the failure of a person in a particular situation, you will want to do everything you can to avoid it. As you determine the cost of a potential failure you will want to compare the cost to the benefit the person may receive from the learning experience.

You will also want to consider the perceptions of the people outside your area and how they will view the failure. Others may not be as enlightened as you in terms of seeing failure as a part of the process of achieving success.

Creating an Environment Where People Aren't Afraid to Fail

Creating an environment where people are not afraid to fail is a difficult task. Again, your job is to reverse ingrained patterns of thinking. Because of prior conditioning, most people are terrified of failure. It will take work on your part to get people to see failure as a positive experience in their lives rather than as something that has the potential to hurt or destroy them.

Here are some of the things you can do to create the kind of environment where people are not afraid to fail.

Provide Guidelines for Failing

If you give people guidelines for failing they will be more comfortable with the idea of taking risks. Even the most inexperienced person knows that there are some failures that will not be tolerated. If you give them guidelines, you'll be more comfortable too. You will have a better basis for reprimanding them when necessary. Here are some suggestions for the kinds of guidelines you may want to set:

- It's okay to make a mistake once, but it is not okay to make the same mistake twice.
- It is okay to fail as long as you try your best.
- If you have serious doubts about what is expected of you, ask for clarification.
- One of the worst kinds of mistakes is inactivity and the failure to make a decision.

Encourage and Reward Risk Taking

Let people know that you want them to take calculated risks. Reassure them that you know they are only human and will make mistakes. Remind them of the quote: "In great attempts it is glorious even to fail." When they take a risk and succeed, give them plenty of praise. Praise them in front of their peers as a way of motivating others to do the same. When they take appropriate risks and fail, acknowledge their courage and their hard work.

Penalize Inactivity and Indecision

As you encourage and reward risk taking, let people know that inactivity and indecision are not acceptable. Let them know that you prefer that they make a decision, even if it is the wrong decision, rather than make no decision at all. Let them know that a record of significant achievement sprinkled with failure is prized far and above a mistake-free record with few achievements.

Let People Know You Make Mistakes

Let your people know that you are human just like them, that you make mistakes too. This is important for them to know because most people have great difficulty tolerating perfection—perhaps it is because perfection mirrors imperfection.

If you want your people to be comfortable with failure and to view it as a positive experience, you must apply the same principles to yourself when you make a mistake.

Through your own actions you can serve as a role model for them on how to use failure as a means of achieving success.

Support People When They Fail

Let your people know that you will be there to catch them when they fall, provided they have followed the guidelines you have set for them. You are their safety net. Reassure them that you will protect them from the "wolves" who might use their failures as opportunities to hurt or discredit them in some way.

Reaffirm People's Self-worth

When people fail, let them know their failure does not diminish their worth as a person or their worth to the department.

For some of your people, when you treat them in this way, you will be acting as the supportive, protective parent they never had. You will be the first person ever to provide them the luxury of being able to fail without being unduly chastised or degraded as a person.

Plan Your Response to Failure

All the guidelines we've provided so far may sound wonderful, but what happens when someone makes a mistake that sends you through the roof? What happens when you want to rip a person apart for having made a mistake, even when he acted within the established guidelines?

First of all, it is important to recognize that those feelings are not a sign of weakness; they simply mean that you are human. The important thing is what you do with those feelings.

If you act on them immediately, more than likely you will destroy any trust you have established between the person and you. Any progress you have made in convincing people that it is okay to fail can be undone in an instant.

You will be better able to accomplish your objectives if you will abide by this unwritten rule: Never reprimand a person unless you are in full control of your own thoughts and emotions. This way you won't say or do things that may result in momentary satisfaction in the short term but regret in the long term.

We aren't suggesting that you never show emotion to your people, that you never let them know you are angry or upset. Showing your people how you feel can be quite beneficial at times, provided it is shown in an appropriate way and for the right reasons.

When you respond constructively to people's failures you are doing the single most important thing you can do to let them know that it is okay to fail.

Never Embarrass a Person in Front of Others

When a person makes a mistake, never reprimand or embarrass him in front of his peers. The fear of being humiliated in front of others is one of the primary reasons why people don't take more risks. Embarrass them once in front of others and the memory of that experience will outweigh anything you could say or do to encourage them to take risks in the future.

Letting People Fail While Enforcing Standards

In Chapter 3, we talked about the importance of setting standards of excellence for people. In this chapter we discussed the importance of giving people permission to fail. To some, these ideas may seem contradictory but in reality they go hand in hand. In order for people to discover and utilize their full potential, they must be given high standards to aim for *and* permission to fail.

The higher the standards, the more important it is that people be given permission to fail. When people are expected to achieve standards of excellence but don't have permission to fail, the standards themselves become stress producers. Excess stress always inhibits productivity and creativity.

If on the other hand people are given permission to fail but there are no standards of excellence, the result will be mediocre work.

When you give people permission to fail it doesn't mean you expect any less of them. Quite the contrary. Because you have given them permission to fail, you have the right to expect even greater achievements from them because they are free to take more risks.

Summary

People must be given permission to fail if they are to fully utilize their own personal power. Here are some guidelines to keep in mind as you grant people permission to fail:

- Help your people see failure as a positive experience.
- Help them minimize their failures by applying the principles in this book.
- Anticipate and plan for failures.
- Weigh the potential cost of each failure.
- Provide people with guidelines for failing.
- Encourage and reward risk taking.
- Penalize inactivity and indecision.
- Let them know that you make mistakes too.
- Stand behind them when they fail.
- Reaffirm their self-worth when they fail.
- Plan your response to failure.
- Never embarrass people in front of their peers.
- Give people permission to fail, but stress the importance of reaching standards of excellence at the same time.

When people are given permission to fail they are able to take greater risks. When they are free of the fear of failure, they are able to devote their energies to achieving the standards of excellence you have set for them. People are more motivated, more creative, and more productive when they know you are there supporting them, particularly when they make a mistake.

The more people stretch and push the limits, the greater the chances are that they will achieve success. The more success people achieve, the more power and success the manager achieves for himself.

CHAPTER

10

POWER THROUGH RESPECT

Power Principle: A manager empowers others by treating them with dignity and respect. When people are treated with respect they have a greater motivation to perform. The motivation to perform must be present if people are to have the power to succeed. The manager has more power to achieve his own objectives when the people who work for him are motivated to achieve success.

The Importance of Respect

Studies show that what most people want in a job above all else is to be treated with respect. Unfortunately, the most commonly practiced crime in industry today is a fundamental insensitivity toward personal dignity.

Successful managers have an ingrained philosophy that says in effect, "Respect the individual," "make people winners," "let people stand out," "treat people as adults." Successful managers reinforce degrees of winning instead of degrees of losing.

Nobody wants to be just a cog in a machine or a number on a payroll. We all want to be treated as a person having worth over and beyond what we can add to the bottom line. A person will never respect or do his best for you if you see him only as a means of getting the job done.

Einstein said it well when he said, "In an age of large-scale events and organizations, the greatest single issue of importance, apart from the question of peace or war, is for the individual to feel that he counts."

Respect and Self-esteem

The respect we show another person can go a long way in building the person's self-esteem. Most of us have fragile egos which need bolstering on a fairly frequent basis. Behind even the most confident façade is usually a person struggling to achieve and/or maintain a feeling of self-worth.

How you treat a person who works for you will affect to some degree how that person feels about himself. And how a person feels about himself will always be reflected in his work.

Respect and common courtesy are the grease that makes for ease of relationships. Without it, the simplest tasks become difficult. Few things deplete energy and reduce productivity faster than a bruised ego.

Usually it's not the big things we say or do to a person that communicate how we feel about him. It's the myriad small things we do and don't do on an everyday basis that communicate very loudly one of two distinct messages—"I respect your rights as an individual and value you as a person" or "You have no rights as a person because I'm the boss and you're the worker. You have value only in terms of what you can contribute to the job."

This perhaps explains why people continue to moan and complain after receiving a promotion and raise. There is no substitute for respect. It is a dominant need shared by all and when it goes unmet, the needs of the job usually go unmet as well.

Ways to Show Respect

Showing respect requires sensitivity to the needs of others. It requires planning and forethought and an understanding of human needs. If this sounds complicated, think of it in terms of the Golden Rule. How do you like to be treated by your boss? Your own needs and desires can be helpful guides for determining how you treat the people who work for you.

There are a thousand and one ways to show respect to a person. It is impossible to list all of them since many are dictated by the needs of the individual and the situation. Actually all 10 Principles for Empowering People which are discussed in this book relate to the issue of respect, which is why I have saved this chapter for the end. When we fail to apply any of these principles, we fail to show respect.

Here are some of the major ways you can show respect for the people who work for you. Some of the ideas are mentioned in other chapters. Since they are so critical to the subject of respect, they are worth repeating. The items on the following pages head the list of employees' most common complaints, which is another reason for making note of them here.

Give Necessary Direction

Tell people what their jobs are in no uncertain terms. If you expect them to be mind readers when it comes to job responsibilities, they will surely interpret your actions as a sign of disrespect.

Provide Adequate Resources

When you give a person the resources to do the job, he will feel that you have taken his needs into consideration. When people are not given the necessary resources, they feel that they are being asked to accomplish the impossible.

Communicate Information on a Timely Basis

When a person doesn't receive the information he needs on time, he is hindered in his ability to do the job and meet deadlines. If he is penalized in any way due to the manager's failure to communicate, he will naturally feel that a great injustice has been done to him.

Delegate Authority Equal to Responsibility

There can be no respect without delegation of authority. When you delegate responsibility but fail to delegate adequate authority, most people will interpret your actions this way: "He wants me to do the job, but he doesn't trust me with the authority I need to get the job done." Failing to delegate proper authority is a blatant show of disrespect for the needs of the person.

Respect People's Time

Why is it that the boss can keep a person waiting but a person dare not keep his boss waiting for even a minute? The waiting game is often nothing more than a power game. When a manager keeps a person waiting outside his office he is com-

municating a subtle message: "I am more important than you. Your job can wait."

Naturally there will be times when you may have to make a person wait. This may happen on occasion, but try to avoid it at all costs. You may boost your own ego by keeping others waiting but you're also losing valuable productivity.

When you give a person an assignment and deadline, make sure you give him enough advance notice. If you dump work on your people and assign deadlines as though everything were an emergency, you will surely have a group of disgruntled people on your hands. Unfair, unrealistic deadlines again communicate a loud message: "He doesn't care about my needs and constraints; he cares only about getting the job done."

Don't Usurp People's Authority

Once you have delegated authority, never take it back unless the person has abused it in some way. As I said before, authority, power, and self-esteem are all tied up together. When you tamper with a person's authority, you are sure to upset the applecart.

Whenever you undermine the authority of people, regardless of your intentions, they will think they have failed in some way, in which case they will lose face in front of others. They will feel that you simply don't care about their feelings and needs.

Look for Ways to Make the Job Easier

One of a manager's primary tasks is clearing away obstacles. A good manager constantly looks for ways he can simplify the work performed by his people.

Some managers seem to do the reverse. They equate complicated systems and a flurry of activity with sophistication and productivity.

When you look for ways to make a person's job easier you get a double benefit. Efficiency and productivity increase and the person thinks you are a saint for relieving him of some of the burdens of the job. Again, he will feel that his needs have been taken into consideration. Once more we are reminded that the needs of the individual and the needs of the company are not mutually exclusive but are interdependent.

Tune into People's Needs

Each person is different, yet everyone shares the same basic needs. We all want respect, but we want to have it expressed in different ways.

If you treat all your people exactly the same, no matter how fair you think you are being, people won't feel that they are getting the respect they deserve. People want to feel special. They want to be recognized as individuals separate from the team.

Unless we understand what makes one person different from the next, unless we understand what makes a person tick, we cannot meet his needs. When a person feels that his needs are being met, he feels that he is respected. When he feels respected, he is more willing to meet the needs of the company.

Listen

Listening is one of the highest forms of respect one person can show another. It says "I value your thoughts and ideas. I want to learn from you." When we listen we give our time and attention, which are two of the most precious gifts we can give to another.

If a person feels that his ideas and thoughts are valued, he will feel valued as a person. If he is ignored and made to feel that he has nothing to contribute, he will have a tendency to live out the message he is receiving.

Provide Adequate Feedback

Feedback is another form of attention. Even if the feedback is constructive criticism, it communicates that you care.

When there is no feedback, the silence will convey messages of its own—messages such as "I don't know what you have been doing or what you have accomplished," "I don't think your work is important enough to comment on," or "I don't really care whether you grow personally or not."

All too often managers fail to give feedback simply because they have difficulty finding the time. You may never intend to communicate any of the above messages. Remember, though, what counts in the long run is the perception of the person, not your intent.

Stand Up for People

A good manager plays many roles, one of which is protector. There is no better way to show your respect for a person than by standing behind him in the heat of battle. When you refuse to let others trample on his dignity and self-respect, even if he has done wrong, you demonstrate the fact that you value him as a person.

Respect People's Privacy

No matter how low a person is within the organization, he has a right to privacy. It is a basic human need and right which is all too often violated in the workplace. As a general rule, the higher one's position, the more privacy one is given. This perhaps explains why so many CEOs are barricaded away from the rank and file.

The demands of some positions do, of course, necessitate greater privacy, and not everyone can have a private office. There are things you can do to respect a person's privacy, regardless of his office environment. If the person has an office with a door, never barge in without knocking. If you enter and he is on the telephone, offer to step outside until he is finished.

If the person doesn't have an office, you'll have to work a little harder at honoring his privacy. If he is talking to another person at his desk or if he is talking on the telephone, don't hover over him. Let him know you would like to see him but let him finish what he is doing. On exceptional occasions you may want to offer the person the use of your private office if he needs to make a confidential phone call or hold a private meeting. When you honor a person's privacy and space in this way, you let the person know that you understand and respect his needs. In the corporate world, privacy is associated with status and importance. If you give a person privacy which he is not usually accorded, he will feel a sense of importance. When a person feels important, he feels respected.

Give People the Right to Express Their Feelings

One of the primary ways we respect another person's feelings is by allowing him to have the feelings in the first place. All too often people believe that if they disagree and/or express negative feelings to the boss, they will be penalized in some way. Their belief is well founded because that is often what happens.

You don't always have to agree with the way another person feels, but you should be willing to listen. If you communicate to a person that you never want to hear any bad news, that you never want to hear a complaint, or that you always want him to be happy and agreeable, you are denying him the right to be who he is. If you operate in this fashion you lose on at least two counts: You may miss out on some valuable information, and you'll have to deal with the low morale that will result from the person's feeling that you don't respect him.

Acknowledge People's Hardships

As a manager you may sometimes have to ask people to endure job-related hardships that are beyond the call of duty. Most people don't mind putting forth the extra effort, provided their sacrifices are acknowledged and appreciated. Sometimes all it takes is a comment or two to satisfy the martyrdom which exists to some degree in almost everyone. When we acknowledge a person's hardships, we acknowledge his needs, which is always a sign of respect.

Respect People's Personal Obligations

You may be a workaholic who devotes every waking moment to the job, but don't expect your people to do the same. There's a great danger in imposing your own work ethic on others. If you consistently ask a person to work late and on weekends without concern for how it is affecting his personal life, he will feel that he is being abused and treated unjustly. An occasional late night, or late nights for a period of time, is reasonable. When it infringes upon his home and family life to an extreme, you've got trouble on your hands. Personal problems resulting from overwork will eventually affect productivity and efficiency.

How to Tell When a Person Feels Disrespected

Just about everything we do or say to a person conveys either respect or disrespect. Respect is the foundation for giving people a sense of power. Therefore, it's important that we be able to recognize when a person doesn't feel he is getting the respect he is due. We cannot go by our good intentions, for what we think we are communicating is often miles away from what the person is actually perceiving.

Some people, of course, will never be satisfied. No matter what we do, some people will feel they are being treated unfairly. These are not the people we are addressing at this point.

Unfortunately, most people rarely come out and say it when they feel they aren't being treated with enough respect. They may act it out in a thousand different ways, but rarely will they put it in those words. For most people, conveying this very personal need would make them too vulnerable in the eyes of their manager. Here are some signs to watch for that may indicate that a person doesn't feel he is getting enough respect:

- The person's productivity declines.
- The quality of the person's work is not up to the standards.
- The person displays a cool or aloof attitude.
- The person is short-tempered.
- The person shows a lack of cooperation.
- The person appears to make errors on purpose.

Whenever a person isn't performing up to the standards, you should ask yourself, "Is the person performing in this way because he doesn't feel he is getting enough respect?" There may be a host of reasons why a person isn't meeting the standards; however, this is always a good starting point.

Here's where the careful observation and sensitivity of the manager is so important. You can answer this question only if you are tuned into the needs of the person. If you make a conscious effort to get to know your people, if you talk with them and counsel them on a regular basis, you will instinctively know when the problem is due to a bruised ego.

Summary

Respect is the foundation for providing people a sense of power. Virtually everything we do or say to a person conveys either respect or disrespect. Here are some ways you can show respect to the people who work for you:

- Provide them with the necessary direction.
- Give them adequate resources.
- Provide them with the information they need on a timely basis.
- Respect their time.
- Don't usurp their authority.
- Look for ways to make their job easier.
- Tune into their needs.
- Listen to them.
- Provide them with feedback.
- Stand up for them.
- Respect their privacy.
- Give them the right to express their feelings.
- Acknowledge their hardships.
- Respect their personal obligations.

When people are treated in this fashion everyone wins. People feel that the manager and company care about them. They have greater self-respect and confidence, which dramatically increases their power to achieve success.

By preserving people's self-respect and dignity the man-

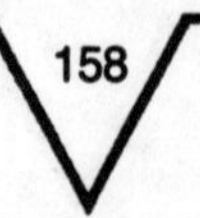

ager wins loyalty and commitment instead of passive cooperation. Loyalty and commitment enable the manager to maximize productivity and efficiency. He's free to concentrate on activities that will lead him to success instead of concentrating on morale problems that occur when people don't feel respected. Motivated people always mean power to the manager.

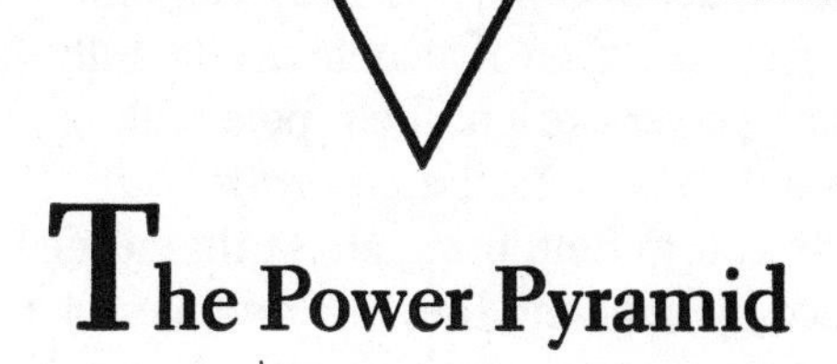

The Power Pyramid

All the ideas we have presented in this book hinge on one central theme: The way to achieve ultimate power as a manager is to give power to the people who work for you.

The 10 Principles for Empowering People which are described in each of the ten chapters of this book provide a total system for giving power to others. These ten principles can best be illustrated through a model which we call the Power Pyramid.

If you apply this model to every person who works for you, you will undoubtedly achieve success as a manager. In order for the model to work, you must not omit a single step. Every step must be taken if people are to fully realize their own personal power, reach their potential, and make the maximum contribution to the company.

We invite you to help bring about the needed changes in the workplace by applying the 10 Principles of Empowering People to the people who work for you. Not only will you be making a significant contribution to the lives of your people and to your company, you will be doing the most important thing you can do to gain power and success for yourself. Remember, if you want it, you have to give it away. Good luck in your pursuit of power.

10 Principles for Empowering People

1. Tell people what their responsibilities are.
2. Give them authority equal to the responsibilities assigned to them.
3. Set standards of excellence.
4. Provide them with training that will enable them to meet the standards.
5. Give them knowledge and information.
6. Provide them with feedback on their performance.
7. Recognize them for their achievements.
8. Trust them.
9. Give them permission to fail.
10. Treat them with dignity and respect.